D1540295

FROM
SCRIPTURE
to THEOLOGY

A Canonical Journey
into Hermeneutics

Charles J. Scalise

InterVarsity Press
Downers Grove, Illinois

InterVarsity Press® is the book-publishing division of InterVarsity Christian Fellowship®, a student movement active on campus at hundreds of universities, colleges and schools of nursing in the United States of America, and a member movement of the International Fellowship of Evangelical Students. For information about local and regional activities, write Public Relations Dept., InterVarsity Christian Fellowship, 6400 Schroeder Rd., P.O. Box 7895, Madison, WI 53707-7895.

Cover photograph: Michael Goss

ISBN 0-8308-1873-1

Printed in the United States of America

Library of Congress Cataloging-in-Publication Data

Scalise, Charles J.
    From scripture to theology: a canonical journey into hermeneutics/
Charles J. Scalise.
      p.   cm.
    Includes bibliographical references.
    ISBN 0-8308-1873-1 (pbk.: alk. paper)
    1. Hermeneutics—Religious aspects—Christianity. 2. Bible—
Canonical criticism. 3. Theology, Doctrinal. I. Title.
BR118.S29 1996
220.6'01—dc20
                                    96-20792
                                        CIP

20	19	18	17	16	15	14	13	12	11	10	9	8	7	6	5	4	3	2	1
12	11	10	09	08	07	06	05	04	03	02	01	00	99	98	97	96			

To my sons David and Daniel

"So when at times the mob is swayed
To carry praise or blame too far,
We may take something like a star
To stay our minds on and be staid."

ROBERT FROST

Preface

Christian students in higher education encounter a bewildering array of scholarly approaches when they seek to study about their faith. Books abound claiming to offer the latest discoveries of critical scholarship, or the newest challenges to the current consensus, or (for the anxious) the same old story that Christians "have always believed."

Perhaps nowhere is the confusion thicker than in the thickets of theology labeled "hermeneutics." This book seeks to offer a readable and reliable guide to a scriptural way through the maze of contemporary reflection and speculation on the problem of how thinking Christians can move from the Bible to doctrine.

This is an introduction to the subject of theological hermeneutics designed for beginning students who possess little or no background in the area. At every point in the text I have sought to render complex ideas in the simplest, reader-friendly language I could find. I am aware that this will inevitably lead to the concern that important subjects have been oversimplified or significant questions ignored. Readers who are interested in a more academically argued, technical approach to the same subject are invited to consult my earlier book, *Hermeneutics as Theological Prolegomena: A Canonical Approach*.

This present work is an intentionally more accessible account, which seeks to make the fruit of research in theological hermeneutics available to a wider audience of students, ministers and educated laity in evangelical Christianity. I have found the discipline of simplifying fine distinctions and subtle arguments for the sake of simpler and clearer communication to be a salutary one despite its inevitable frustrations. I have compiled a detailed, annotated bibliography to the field so that interested students and teachers may further pursue the subjects raised.

The journey of writing this book has indeed been a pilgrimage with many encouragers and exhorters along the way. William Hendricks, formerly at The Southern Baptist Theological Seminary and now at Texas Christian University, guided and encouraged my graduate study in the area of theological hermeneutics. Research for the bibliography which accompanies this book was begun under his direction and represents the product of a continuing collaboration. Also, his skill in popularizing and communicating contemporary theological issues to generations of college and seminary students has been a guiding light in my teaching and in this work.

David Dockery, president of Union University in Jackson, Tennessee, initially encouraged me in this project. As my former faculty colleague and dean at Southern Seminary, he maintained that Baptists and other evangelicals were ready for clear, straightforward discussion of contemporary issues in hermeneutics. I fervently share his hope for a welcome reception of this discussion of some biblical and theological matters on which there has been much heat and little light.

Dan Stiver, professor of Christian philosophy at Southern Seminary, has been a fellow traveler and the best of colleagues in my journey through the process of learning to think hermeneutically about Christian theology. In the 1989-1990 academic year Dan and I, with colleagues Craig Loscalzo and David Dockery, began a hermeneutics study group that encouraged me to sharpen my own views through cross-disciplinary dialogue with group members and various other contemporary scholars. Dan and I continued our hermeneutical conversations during 1990-1991, while he was studying at Tübingen and I was at Regent's Park College at the University of Oxford.

On returning to Southern Seminary, we revitalized our hermeneutics study group and proposed an interdisciplinary course, which we team taught with colleagues John Watts (Old Testament) and Craig Loscalzo (Christian preaching). This experiment provided valuable experience in communicating my views on historical and theological aspects of biblical hermeneutics to a diverse group of seminarians. In addition, Dan and Professor Amy Plantinga Pauw of Louisville Presbyterian Theological Seminary read most of the chapters of this book in draft form in a study group that provided much stimulation and support for completing this work.

Southern Seminary students Gary Conner and Dan Davis, who also have shared in the fellowship of the Charis Sunday-school class at St. Matthews Baptist Church, graciously consented to read the entire manuscript in draft form. Their helpful, practical suggestions have made this book clearer and more user-friendly for students.

My colleagues in the church history department at Fuller Theological Seminary—James Bradley, Cecil M. Robeck Jr., John Thompson and Daryl Fisher-Ogden—generously offered insight and additional resources as they reviewed my efforts to reshape the second chapter for a broader evangelical audience. Sharing in the department's community of hospitality and learning has enriched my writing.

The support of William A. Dyrness, dean of Fuller Seminary's School of Theology, was vital in assisting me to bring this work to publication. My Seattle colleagues Richard Erickson and Timothy Dearborn also provided sympathetic understanding of the challenges and demands of writing for publication. Jan Wessman offered faithful clerical assistance.

Daniel G. Reid, academic and reference books editor for InterVarsity, enthusiastically adopted and gently shepherded this project through the publishing process. His insights and modifications skillfully shaped this work into its final form.

My gratitude for all of these persons who have played important roles in the journey of writing this book should be accompanied by a disclaimer of their responsibility for any meandering byways or dead ends that remain. If readers find themselves lost or confused on this hermeneutical road, I am the one who is to blame for giving bad directions!

The partnership of love, learning and life which I share with my wife Pamela has nurtured this study in countless visible and hidden ways. As we have journeyed west to become members of the Fuller Seminary faculty, the completion of this project offers an expectant overture to the new venture of ministry unfolding before us. In this hope begotten of our abiding faith in God, we are grateful for David and Daniel, our special "heritage from the Lord," to whom this book is dedicated.

1. Beginning the Journey
From Bible to Doctrine

T HE CALL TO FOLLOW JESUS Christ is an invitation to a life of pilgrimage. One of the earliest names for Christianity is simply "the road" or "the Way" (Acts 19:23). Throughout our Christian lives the obedience of faith is not simply an undertaking of our hearts, but also of our minds (cf. Mt 22:37). Bonaventure, one of the great thinkers of the Middle Ages, pictures this dimension of Christian spirituality as "The Mind's Road to God."[1]

This book invites its readers to embark on a theological journey. Traveling this way can enable us to grow spiritually as Christians. We want to learn to love God more deeply with our minds. Our pilgrimage will begin with the Bible and move to Christian doctrine. We will be particularly concerned with the question of how Christians can traverse the distance between Scripture and doctrine with intellectual integrity. In other words, how do we start from the written Word of God in the Bible and end up with the doctrines of the faith?

Before we begin a long journey, we need to take stock and make plans and preparations. Let's first pause and consider our reasons for making the journey and our route through the territory that lies ahead. Why are we making this trip? Do we need to make such a journey? From where are we starting? What should we take along with us? How do we plan to get to our destination? Which roads will we take and what do we expect to encounter along the way?

This chapter is devoted to responding to these sorts of questions. We will begin with an introduction to the nature of our theological journey. We will discuss what theology is and how certain ways of thinking theologically can help Christians move from the words of Scripture to the language of doctrine. Then we will undergo some "travel orientation." We will think about the matter of our theological point of view and its influence on our making the journey.

Next we will spend some time packing for the trip, as we examine some theological presuppositions which will play a major role in shaping the way the trip goes. Since we are traveling from Scripture to doctrine, we will be particularly concerned to define what we mean by the authority of the former and the nature of the latter.

Following this packing-up time, we will turn our attention to our means of transportation. We will be introduced to the idea of hermeneutics. (See the discussion of "The Mode of Transportation" later in this chapter for a definition.) In addition, we will become acquainted with the make (theological hermeneutics) and model (canonical hermeneutics) of the particular vehicle we will be using on the trip.

The last section of this chapter will be devoted to looking ahead and charting the course of our journey, offering a brief overview of the rest of the book.

At the end of this book is an introductory, annotated bibliography of the field of theological hermeneutics. During the course of our journey, I will be referring in the notes to particular writers and works on whom I am dependent. (Works marked in the notes with an asterisk [*] before the title will be found in the bibliography with additional information.) The notes seek to offer a guide to specific authors, titles and sections in the bibliography. Readers interested in pursuing a particular topic further (for example, for a research paper) are invited to consult the bibliography for related works and additional information and discussion.

The Nature of the Journey: Thinking Theologically
The word *theology* derives from two Greek words: (1) *theos* meaning "god" and (2) *logos* meaning "word" or "reason." Therefore, ety-

mologically *theology* signifies talking or reasoning (thinking) about God. This simple definition, however, is not the entire story. While theology necessarily requires thinking and talking about God, not all talk and thought about God is theology. On the one hand, thinking about God may be so abstract and remote that it is irrelevant to one's life and religious community. Instead, theology requires a self-involving response. Christian theology should impact our personal faith and shape our churches and fellowship groups.

On the other hand, thinking theologically is not identical with all of the words we use in our day-to-day religious communication. When Christians read the Bible, pray or give a testimony, they are talking and thinking about God, but they aren't doing theology. (There will be an implicit theology which underlies what they are saying and doing, but this is not the same thing as intentional theological reflection.)

Activities like reading the Bible, praying and giving a testimony are what philosophers call primary or *first-order* religious language. Doing theology involves secondary or *second-order* religious language. Christians reflect on the uses of primary religious language in the Bible, worship, prayer and other Christian activities. Thus theological language is second-order language—talk about God that thinks about the ways people have thought and talked about God throughout the centuries.

Christian theology involves more than just repeating, restating and reorganizing a collection of assertions gleaned from the Bible. Such a view of theology can (often unconsciously and unintentionally) reduce the Bible to a stack of propositions which somehow must be harmonized so all the "biblical difficulties" disappear. Theology becomes simply a collation of facts selected from the Bible. Christians who hold this view may miss much of the spiritual depth and richness of the Bible by reading it something like a cookbook or a science book. Their propositions about the Bible can make reading it a somewhat mechanical process, rather than a spiritual one. (We might say that they have a "flat" Bible.) The mystery and power of Scripture—its character as "treasure in earthen vessels" (2 Cor 4:7 RSV)—is lost if it is interpreted only as a series of facts to be believed and orders to be obeyed.

If theology is not just the collection of Bible facts and their rearrangement, then what is it? *Christian theology is the church's critical self-examination of the language it uses to speak of the mystery of God.* If there is anything we know about God, it is that God is greater than anything we try to say about God. So-called "philosophical proofs" for the existence of God (like Anselm's famous ontological argument) have their practical theological value in the ways they describe our language about God, not in their capability to prove that God is. If proofs could really do the latter, then God would become a function of the proofs, instead of vice versa. Our finite human minds and time-bound human language cannot even completely grasp, let alone prove, the mystery of the eternal God.

If anyone claims that he or she has God all figured out and wrapped up in a nice neat package, then we can be sure that the God in that box is too small. The package may contain a god—but it is an idol of human creation, not the living God of the Bible. (The Arian bishop Eunomius, who claimed to know God as well as God knows Godself, offers an ancient example of this kind of theological arrogance.) All of our language ultimately breaks down before the mystery of God. Martin Luther pictures us as babes babbling before the great divine mystery.

Christian language about God walks a tightrope between two opposing pitfalls. There is the danger of our language about God becoming too abstract and esoteric—too removed from the struggles and sufferings of everyday life. The Incarnation—the Word made flesh in Jesus—calls us away from this danger. But there is also the danger of our language about God becoming too familiar and trivializing. Instead of remembering that we are speaking of the Creator of the universe, we talk about God like a cosmic bellhop, who exists only to do our bidding.

We are called to talk about God. Yet Christian theology challenges us to "watch our language" about God. The language Christians use when they address God in public prayer often particularly reveals much of their working understanding of God. ("The law of praying is the law of believing"—in Latin, *lex orandi, lex credendi*—is the way an ancient theological slogan describes this situation.) Theology invites Christians to examine carefully the ways they speak to God as well as the ways they speak about God. Christian theology puts to the test all of the language we use regarding God.

What is the test which theology puts to our inadequate words about almighty God? Ultimately, our words are tested against the living Word of God, Jesus Christ, for Christian theology is one area of the church's ministry in the name of Jesus Christ. Operationally, theology tests our language about God against the written Word of God in Scripture. Since the Bible must be interpreted both by individual Christians and by communities of faith, our personal experience of Christian faith and the historical traditions of Christian communities also have important roles to play in the process. We will examine these complex relationships later in this chapter in a discussion of our theological presupposition of the authority of Scripture. Before we turn to that matter of theological "packing for our journey," however, we must first deal with some issues of orientation for the trip.

Travel Orientation: The Theological Point of View

If theology is the church's *self-examination* of its language, then the language of theology is "insider's language." In other words, theological discussions are principally "in-house" discussions, where Christians, who believe and trust in God's promises and presence, engage one another about the teachings (doctrines) of their faith. In essence, theology involves Christians loving God with all their minds (Mt 22:37, Mk 12:30 and Lk 10:27). Christian doctrine is not primarily a debate with the world about God, but a conversation about God among the members of the household of faith.

Of course, there are many occasions when Christians talk about their faith to others outside Christianity, but those sorts of discussions fall into categories like apologetics (defending and/or explaining the faith to nonbelievers) or evangelism and missions, rather than Christian doctrine. Thus theological language has the immediate purpose of helping Christians to understand God's gift of faith more clearly and deeply, rather than proving Christianity to others. If Christians are more deeply grounded in their faith, then the church will be able to carry out its mission to the world (Mt 28:19-20).

Anselm of Canterbury receives the credit for formulating the slogan which best expresses the point of view of theological language. Anselm declared that Christian theology is "faith seeking under-

Theology is not apologetics

standing" (*fides quaerens intellectum*). Christians approach the theological task with the assumption of faith and the goal of understanding. Theology doesn't work by first enabling someone on the outside to understand all about the faith and only then to believe it. The movement is not from understanding all about the mystery of God to the experience of faith. Rather, Christian theology begins from the inside with the gift of faith and then seeks to move to understanding more of the mystery of God.

The theological point of view of faith seeking understanding calls us to humility before the greatness and mystery of God. Any Christian theologian who claims to have understood everything about God has misunderstood the faith. (He or she stands in the heretical tradition of Eunomius.) Any Christian theology that claims to be able to *prove* its understanding of God to an unbelieving world has missed the starting point of faith. Christian theology moves from faith to understanding, not from understanding to faith.

Whose faith does theology assume as its starting point? Is it simply the faith of the individual Christian who is trying to do theology? Is it some standard of theological interpretation (like a creed) that was created by Christians long ago? Although personal faith and historical monuments to the faith of others play their role, the starting point lies in *living communities of faith.* The worship, teaching and mission of the Christian church create the contexts in which faith begins. Christian theology is done on behalf of and in service toward the church—communities of believers today who are connected down through the ages with the people of God.

Doing Christian theology from the starting point of one's individual faith alone is inadequate for two reasons. First, it ignores the truth that most of what one has experienced about the faith has been learned from others. For instance, when one accepts Jesus Christ as Lord, others from the Christian community introduce the new Christian to the faith. Second, starting from one's individual faith alone ignores the limitations posed by one's own sinfulness. Acting as if one's own experience is the only valid point of departure is an act of theological arrogance. Christians doing theology need the checks and balances offered by the experience of others—both past and present—in communities of faith.

Doing Christian theology from the starting point of the historical faith of others alone is also inadequate. Such a view makes Christian theology into a historical investigation of the Christian tradition. The language of theology then becomes the language of the detached observer. The personal faith of the theologian becomes irrelevant to the task, and theology is divorced from the life of the church. Faith is reduced to the record of the past experience of others. Faith becomes only an inheritance from the past or an adoption of someone else's religious experience.

Therefore the starting point for the theological point of view that moves from faith to understanding lies within the life of communities of faith. Personal faith and historical tradition are inextricably intertwined in the task of seeking clearer and deeper understanding.

The kind of understanding that theology seeks is neither a collection of cut-and-dried facts arranged with an air of false objectivity, nor is it a sentimentalized conglomeration of religious emotions culled from the experience of believers. Rather, theological understanding expresses the ongoing quest for our personal knowledge of God.

There is a sort of knowing that can only be attained through loving and being loved. One can glimpse something of this sort of transforming love in a special lifelong friendship or a good, long-standing marriage, where the partners grow toward one another to the point that it is hard to imagine the one without the other. In such a situation, the goal of understanding the other is never fully attained, but always deepened.

Theology which moves from faith to understanding never can claim completely to achieve its goal. Each generation seeks to enrich its knowledge of God based on its contemporary experience of faith and the historical traditions left by those who have gone before, interpreted by the norm of Scripture. The understanding which faith seeks is not a possession that can be controlled, but a gift of God's grace that calls for our gratitude.

Faith seeking understanding provides us with a perspective or point of view on the theological task which serves as a general orientation for our journey from Bible to doctrine. Having explored this travel orientation, it is now time to face the challenge of packing for our trip.

Packing: Our Theological Presuppositions

What one chooses to pack for a trip reveals much about one's expectations and one's situation at the starting point. For our journey we will be packing some important theological assumptions or presuppositions that will shape the rest of our travel. Philosophers call these sort of assumptions "basic beliefs." They are presuppositions that constitute our point of departure, as well as shaping the agenda which will be important to us along the way. Every journey must start somewhere, and these beliefs mark out how and where we are starting. We are not seeking to prove these presuppositions; they are the basic assumptions which describe the kind of travelers we are.

The authority of Scripture. The Bible, including both the Old and New Testaments, is recognized and read as the Holy Scripture of the Christian faith. Taken together the Scriptures constitute the canon, the rule which governs the teachings of the faith. Christians claim that God has spoken and continues to speak to us through these books. Because God *speaks* to us when we read the Bible as Holy Scripture, Christians accept the Bible as the written *Word* of God. The Bible used as canonical Scripture becomes uniquely authoritative for Christian belief and practice.

One way that theologians have described this special authority is to call Scripture the "norm-making norm" or "rule-making rule" *(norma normans)* of the faith. The Bible is the rule by which all the other traditions of the faith are judged. In contrast to the Scriptures, all other authorities are only "normed norms" *(norma normata).* In other words, all other sources of religious authority are subordinate to and must be tested against the truth of the Bible.

Subordinate to the rule of Scripture are two other sources of authority for the Christian life: the Christian community and personal experience. When one professes faith in Jesus Christ, this commitment is expressed in response to the witness of the Christian community. One hears the gospel—the good news of the story of Jesus—from other Christians who are members of the Christian community. Certainly it is hypothetically possible that one could be alone on a desert island, find a Bible and be gloriously saved. That, however, is not the way most people become Christians. Moreover, even if one were converted in such an unusual manner, he or she would be relying on members of the Christian community who preserved, translated and printed that Bible. Therefore the Christian community—both through its historical traditions and in its contemporary forms—always remains a source of authority for our lives as Christians. *tough for some to swallow*

The Bible must continually be interpreted in the community of believers. God continues to speak in old and new ways through the Scriptures to the people of God. The interpretation of Scripture is always finally a community activity, rather than just a private one (cf. 2 Pet 1:20). All claims that God is speaking a particular message to a specific person or group through a passage of Scripture should be tested by the Christian community. Without such testing all sorts of manipulation and delusion will be perpetrated in the name of biblical interpretation.

The other additional source of authority for the Christian life, under the primacy of Scripture, is personal experience. Christians confess Jesus Christ as their *personal* Lord and Savior. Salvation is dependent on a personal encounter with God through Jesus Christ. The truth of the Christian faith must become truth for me—the guiding truth of my own life. Without the authority of personal experience, Christianity may be viewed as a religious tradition or cultural heritage, but it cannot become one's living faith.

Therefore under the authority of God as revealed in Jesus Christ, there are three sources of authority for the Christian life—and thus for Christian theology. The first source is Scripture—the written Word of God. Under the primacy of Scripture are two other sources of authority—the Christian community and personal experience. All three sources are needed for a mature and balanced Christian life.

The inexhaustibility of Scripture. The second basic presupposition which we will pack for our journey relates to our practical experience in the reading of Scripture. Christians believe that the Bible is the divinely inspired Word of God. This claim, of course, includes the recognition that the Bible—like classic works of all kinds[2]—is able to speak across generations and cultural groups. The Bible is an inspired work of literature that portrays truth across the ages—like Homer's epics or Shakespeare's plays. The Christian claim that the Bible is *divinely* inspired, however, goes far beyond this view. Christians believe that *God speaks* to God's people through the Scriptures.

The Bible is the Word of God because God speaks through it. (Our individual and community-based experiences of hearing God speak to us through the reading of Scripture do not constitute the Bible as the Word of God, but provide a context where God's Word can be heard.) God has spoken to the people of God in the past through the Scriptures, and God continues to speak to us today through the Scriptures.

The Christian belief that the Bible is the Word of God does not depend on some human theory about its composition. Christians know that the Bible is the *Word* of God because, when they come to the Bible with all their needs and concerns, *God speaks to them* as they read it or hear it read. The Scriptures are an inexhaustible resource and source of authoritative guidance for the people of God. As the famous slogan attributed to the Puritan John Robinson concisely confesses, "God hath yet more light to be revealed in His Holy Word." Both the historical traditions of the Christian community and the personal experience of the Christian believer witness to this practical reality upon which the authority of Scripture rests. Hearing God speak through the Bible points to the need for continual interpretation of the Scriptures.

All theological declarations about the inspiration of the Bible may be understood as human efforts to explain the reality that God has spoken and continues to speak to the people of God through the Scriptures. The inexhaustible light which the Scriptures offer to members of the Christian community who read them and use them as a sure guide to life is the practical, underlying reality which undergirds and tests the assertions Christians make about the nature and status of the Bible.

This critical evaluative role of Scripture becomes clearly manifest in its connection with the formulation of Christian doctrine. The final theological presupposition which we must pack for our hermeneutical journey describes the nature and development of this doctrinal language.

The nature and development of doctrine. Christian doctrine is the use of second-order religious language by members of the Christian community to describe the basic teachings of the faith in the most coherent fashion possible. Christian doctrine is insider's language, though others from outside the Christian community are welcome to listen in on the conversation. Beginning from and tested by Scripture, doctrine seeks to order and reflect on the major themes of the faith.

At the heart of the Christian faith are great mysteries which no Christian should claim to understand completely—the mystery of the triune God, the mystery of the Incarnation (the Word become flesh in Jesus Christ), the mystery of our salvation through Christ's death and resurrection. Christian doctrine does *not* seek to explain these mysteries. Instead, doctrine serves to provide boundary markers for the mysteries; doctrine specifies the limits within which Christians may regulate their speech about God and the teachings of their biblical faith. *I'm not so sure about this - I would think*

Consider the doctrine of the Trinity, the one God in three "persons"—the Father, the Son and the Holy Spirit.[3] Christian doctrine offers two negative guidelines which serve as boundary markers. The first negative guideline says that Christians should not say the Father, Son and Holy Spirit are three separate Gods (three individual centers of God). Such a view (tritheism) would be the sort of polytheism condemned by Scripture (e.g., Deut 6:4). The second negative guideline says that God is not an undifferentiated monolith. That sort of view would ignore the biblical witness to the threeness of God as Father, Son and Spirit.

Christian doctrine marks out the territory within which we can legitimately explore the relationship between the oneness and threeness of God. Christian doctrine does not explain the mystery of the Trinity. Doctrine does not tell us specifically how to relate the threeness of God to the oneness of God. Rather, doctrine offers us *rules* (negative guidelines), which mark out the boundaries within which we can struggle to glimpse the mystery of God's three-in-oneness. Doctrine provides the rule that Christians cannot think adequately about God's threeness apart from God's oneness, and also the rule that we cannot think adequately about God's oneness apart from God's threeness.

These rules about the mystery of the triune God are not found in the Bible, although they are congruent with what the Bible says about God. The rules of the Christian doctrine of the Trinity *developed* during the first four centuries of the Christian church, as Christians tried to make sense of the Bible's teaching and their experience of

these 'boundaries' are discovered in the process of theology

God. The understanding of God as Trinity went through a long process of historical shaping. The climax of this development may be found in the Nicene-Constantinopolitan Creed of A.D. 381, which formulated the official language of the early church about the doctrine of the Trinity.

In summary, Christian doctrine consists of rules which have been developed through the centuries by Christian communities to bound the great mysteries of the faith. This doctrinal development particularly occurred as Christians tried to preserve their faith in the midst of controversies over alternative explanations which often proved heretical. Doctrine does not explain the mysteries. Instead, it offers us boundaries within which we can legitimately reflect on the meaning(s) of the great teachings of our faith.

We have now completed the packing of our three basic theological presuppositions: (1) the primacy of Scripture, (2) the inexhaustibility of Scripture and (3) the regulative nature and historical development of doctrine. We next will explore our means of transportation.

The Mode of Transportation: Canonical Hermeneutics

In order to make our journey from Scripture to doctrine we need to have a means of transportation. In this book our general area of concern will be with the field of theological hermeneutics. Our specific focus will be on the subject of canonical hermeneutics.

Hermeneutics is a field that has been defined in a host of ways.[4] For our purposes, the simple definition that hermeneutics is the theory of the interpretation of texts[5] will be adequate, although *text* may be expanded to include other things beside written materials. For instance, one may be said to "read" a pattern of behavior or a series of human actions.[6]

Theological hermeneutics refers to the approaches (both explicit and implicit) which religious communities have used to interpret sacred texts. For Christians theological hermeneutics specifically focuses on the ways in which the Bible preeminently and the traditions of the Christian community secondarily have been interpreted as authoritative for Christian faith and practice.

Canonical hermeneutics refers specifically to one of the recent approaches to the interpretation of the Bible. A canonical approach emphasizes that the Christian community has recognized this particular collection of books as canon—the rule which guides and tests our beliefs and actions. Christians read the Bible as *Scripture,* God's written word to the people of God.

Christians should not understand the Bible as simply a collection of some ancient texts, like one might do in a university class on the history of the Near East or the Greco-Roman classical world. Neither should Christians regard the Bible as solely a book of inspiring literature, like one might analyze in a course on great world literature. Christians also should not read the Bible as merely a conglomeration of scientific and historical facts, which one might use as "proof" in a debate over the truth of Christianity. Rather, Christians should (and have indeed historically) read the Bible as possessing a unique pattern of theological and practical authority for their lives, both individually and as a community.

The canonical approach which we will use for our journey from Scripture to doctrine was first developed by Brevard S. Childs. Childs set forth his proposal in two technical introductions to the fields of biblical interpretation: *Introduction to the Old Testament as Scripture*[7] and *The New Testament as Canon: An Introduction.*[8] I will describe in greater detail Childs's canonical approach in the third chapter of this book. In addition, based on criticisms which Childs's approach has received, we will make some modifications, as we seek to develop a refined version of canonical hermeneutics for our journey from Scripture to doctrine.

Charting the Course: An Overview

What is our travel plan? What is the course we will be following in the remainder of this book? Since we are by no means the first generation of Christians to struggle with the journey from Scripture to doctrine, we must first spend some time examining the routes that others have used to make the trip. During the centuries since the Enlightenment, thinking Christians have sought to approach the journey through a doctrine of revelation which raises the problem of the relationship between the Bible and history. In the next chapter we will be particularly examining two different models that Christians have used to tie together the Bible and history: one which sees the Bible as the source of all the "facts" of revelation and the other which sees the Bible as the historical record of the "events" of revelation. I will seek to show the problems that each of these models raises for making the journey from Scripture to doctrine today. Underlying both of these models are some difficulties in their use of the doctrine of revelation, which is responsible for some of the "breakdowns" along the road.

The third chapter examines the new route for our journey provided by canonical hermeneutics. Childs's canonical approach to biblical interpretation is described, and specific examples of its usefulness for understanding the Scriptures are provided. Then I suggest several modifications of Childs's proposal to clarify and strengthen canonical hermeneutics as the vehicle for our travel.

Next we turn to the task of exploring the surroundings of theological method. The fourth chapter argues that canonical hermeneutics provides Christians with an effective way to appropriate the entire history of biblical interpretation—both "precritical" and "critical"— for the shaping of Christian doctrine. Canonical hermeneutics moves beyond the limitations of both the facts-of-revelation and the events-of-revelation models.

We glimpse the destination of our journey in the fifth chapter. As we move toward a canonical model of Christian doctrine, we consider some of the implications of this new approach for our scriptural understanding of the doctrine of God.

Having packed our bags and surveyed the journey that lies ahead, we are now ready to traverse the old roads of the relationship between the Bible and history.

2. Investigating Old Roads
The Bible & History

WHENEVER CHRISTIANS STUDY the Bible and seek to interpret its meanings for life, they are not alone. The presence of God the Holy Spirit has enlivened the pages of Scripture for generations of the people of God. If Christians are to discern rightly the truth of the Bible, they need to learn from the encounters of those who have preceded them on the interpretive journey. Therefore history is an indispensable partner in our quest for hermeneutics.[1]

The story about the history of the interpretation of the Bible is an intricate and entangling one.[2] It is inextricably interwoven with the history of the Christian church in the various periods and across the diverse cultures in which Christian communities have flourished and declined.[3] Much of this story of biblical hermeneutics plays a major role in shaping our Christian identity; some aspects, however, are simply fascinating byways or even dead-end streets! For example, the uncontrolled allegorical flights of fancy which characterized the extremes of Origen's and other Alexandrian exegesis in the early church point to such an interpretive dead end.[4] In the fourth chapter we will be exploring some ways in which canonical hermeneutics enables us to appropriate some of the contributions of earlier eras of interpretation without ignoring their limitations.

In this chapter we will be focusing on approaches relating the Bible and history which have characterized many evangelical Christians in the twentieth century. In particular we will be looking at two models that have been widely advocated in both serious discussion and popular rhetoric among evangelicals concerning the Bible and theology. The first one we will simply call the "facts-of-revelation" model. The second one we will label the "events-of-revelation" model.

Each of these models proposes a route for our journey between the Bible and Christian doctrine. A number of thinking, deeply committed Christians have taken each route. They have encountered, however, some sizeable spiritual and intellectual obstacles along the way.[5]

After examining briefly the strengths and limitations of each of these models, we will turn our attention to a deeper source of the inadequacies of both of these approaches: the "breakdown" of the traditional understanding of the doctrine of revelation.

The Facts-of-Revelation Route

Our exploration of the facts-of-revelation route from the Bible to Christian doctrine will first describe this model as set forth by some of its popular defenders. Then we will examine some of the major obstacles it encounters as raised by its critics.

Description. Christians who take this route understand Christian doctrine to be the organization and arrangement of facts, which have already been collected in the Bible. During the American Enlightenment the Common Sense realism of Scottish philosophers like Thomas Reid (1710-1796) shaped this approach.[6] As the stalwart Old Princeton theologian Charles Hodge declared, the Bible is a "storehouse of facts."[7] All the facts that theology needs may be found in the Bible. It is the task of the theologian to organize scientifically the data of the Bible into doctrinal propositions.

The journey from Bible to doctrine follows a straight and clear path. One begins with the data from the Bible and, guided by the Holy Spirit, arranges it into (or logically discovers within it) the rational propositions of Christian doctrine.[8] The facts are all given in the Bible. Doctrines simply systematize the facts.

In this approach the truth of the facts of the Bible is guaranteed by the doctrine of the inspiration of Scripture. Because God inspired the

Bible we know that all the facts in it are true. God's inspiration of the Bible requires belief in the historical accuracy of all its details. If one fact should prove to be questionable or wrong, then the entire Bible is vulnerable to attack. The Bible stands or falls as a unified collection of facts. When reduced to the language of bumper-sticker theology, such a view may find itself asserting, "The Bible says it. I believe it. That settles it!"

ouch!

Following this route commonly promotes a "give them the facts and they will make a decision" approach to Christian commitment. If we just give people the facts about Christianity in our preaching and teaching, then they will have a rational basis for deciding for or against Christ. The Bible is historical "evidence that demands a verdict."[9] Faith is based on understanding the facts about Jesus, but which facts? How do all of the facts fit together?

This fact-centered view of the nature of the Bible encourages its defenders to attempt to harmonize every detail of the biblical accounts. (Gleason Archer's *Encyclopedia of Biblical Difficulties*[10] is one of the more monumental examples.) Chronologies of the life and ministry of Jesus, cock crowings at the time of Simon Peter's denial (cf. Mt 26:34, 74-75; Mk 14:30, 68, 72; Lk 22:34, 60-61; Jn 13:38; 18:27) and even varying accounts of the method of Judas Iscariot's suicide (cf. Mt 27:5 and Acts 1:18) must all precisely fit together. The truth of the Scripture and the historical accuracy of its details are commonly seen as one inseparable issue.

Obstacles. Critics of the facts-of-revelation route are quick to point out the ambiguity of the idea of "facts." Even contemporary scientists are reluctant to claim that one can have facts apart from theory. Facts are "theory-laden." Physics—with its quantum mechanics and Heisenberg uncertainty principle—talks about indeterminacy and probability instead of fixed laws of nature. The light by which we can read this book sometimes functions like a wave and sometimes like a particle. Thus, the "facts" seem to change with context.

Historical facts are dependent on their context.[11] They do not exist in isolation. The very language in which they are composed contains conventions (e.g., numbers, calendars) and ways of seeing the world which must be interpreted. The kind of literature (or other medium) in which they are found provides a surrounding context that shapes their meaning. For instance, we would read the historical description of a person's life as inscribed on a family tombstone with a different eye than that contained in a polemic written by one of his or her bitterest enemies! Furthermore, the broader culture plays a large role in determining what historical facts are considered worth remembering and preserving and what should be consigned to oblivion.

Contemporary philosophers[12] have pointed to the importance of context in shaping the meaning of language. For instance, confessing "Jesus is Lord" when the context declares "Caesar is Lord" adds a new and risky dimension to the meaning of the early Christians' statement of faith. The meanings of words are not fixed forever in some isolated vacuum. They are shaped by the ways in which those who speak the language use them.

A significant obstacle to the facts-of-revelation route is that the original contexts of biblical texts were not monolithic. Consider the different ways in which Jesus' quotations or allusions to the Old Testament text could be heard by his contemporaries, as well as by the Gospel writers.[13] As we can see from the existence of *four* Gospels, Jesus' words (and also his deeds) were perceived by his disciples in different ways. God speaks to us through the diversity of the Scripture.

All of this dependence of facts upon context is further complicated by the existence of multiple, changing contexts.[14] To continue our example, when we read a passage from the Gospels in which Jesus is quoting or alluding to an Old Testament text, we suddenly are faced with a great variety of levels or "horizons" on which these words have different meanings. First, there are the traditions which, guided by the providence of God, led to the formation of this text and its inclusion in the Hebrew Bible. Next, one must consider the various ways in which God spoke first to Jews and later to Christians through this text in relation to other texts in the Old Testament. Then the context in which Jesus used this text must be carefully examined, along with the situation(s) of the Gospel writer(s) and their audience(s) who, guided by the inspiration of God, included Jesus' use of the text in the books that became the New Testament.

Following this level are the enormous variety of contexts in which persons have read and interpreted this New Testament text across the different periods of the history of Christianity: the early church, the

Middle Ages, the Renaissance and Reformation, the modern period.[15] Also, the different cultures and locations in society of various biblical interpreters (e.g., members of the political establishment vs. members of a persecuted minority) must be taken into account.[16] Finally, at the end of this entire process is our own contemporary context.

Therefore if we seek to determine the "historical facts," we face the significant obstacle of searching through an exhausting array of horizons of meaning, each of which has helped to shape (or deform) the meaning of the words in the text we are considering. Each of these levels acts something like a filter through which we try to peer to discern earlier contexts. Unfortunately, even if we could successfully discover the original context(s), our journey to the historical facts is not at an end. Another obstacle still stands in the way.

This obstacle is ourselves in our own context.[17] We hear Jesus' words through the language, personalities and culture which we bring to the text. We bring to the gospel text an idea of "historical facts" influenced by the European Enlightenment, which may be quite different from the way Jesus and his disciples perceived what happened in their world.[18] Any historical research involves a process of selection and interpretation of materials. The perceptions and presuppositions, both conscious and unconscious, which the historian brings to the task act like lenses which screen and shape how the sources are viewed and interpreted.[19] Despite the historian's best efforts to compensate for his or her biases, they will inevitably influence the selection process. Imagine, for example, an account of the exodus from an Egyptian perspective!

The facts-of-revelation route, although initially seeming quite straightforward, has proven to be much more complex and beset with obstacles. When it is not clear precisely what constitutes a fact and what processes of interpretation will generate reliable historical data, evangelical Christians have good reason to wonder whether the road of the facts of revelation is the best way to make the journey from the inspired truth of the Bible to Christian doctrine.

The Events-of-Revelation Route

In an effort to respond to the challenges raised by the historical critical study of the Bible, many committed Christian scholars of the twentieth century have attempted to take another route in the journey of relating the Bible and Christian doctrine. This route seeks to include the results of scholarly research on the Bible while emphasizing the role of the community of faith in biblical interpretation. The facts-of-revelation route lacks this focus on the role of the community of faith in the ongoing process of the writing, editing, compiling and interpretation of Scripture.

Description. The doctrine of revelation is of key importance in the events-of-revelation route. Revelation is a life-transforming event, not just the mere transmittal of information. The word *revelation* carries the picture of unveiling something. "To reveal" involves making known something that has been secret or hidden.

According to the events-of-revelation model, history is the arena for God's self-revelation. Revelation is the *saving acts of God in history.* The heart of what God is doing in history is saving God's people, not just inspiring the biblical account of salvation. So revelation is understood as the history of salvation.[20] (The German term *Heilsgeschichte,* reflecting the formulation of this idea by German scholars such as Oscar Cullmann,[21] is commonly used to describe this approach.)

The Bible, according to the events-of-revelation route, is not the primary revelation itself, but the *record* of God's revelation in history. Specifically, the Bible contains the witness to God's saving acts in history. As G. Ernest Wright declared, the Bible is "the book of the acts of God."[22] When Christians turn to the Bible, they interpret it by faith.

Unlike the facts-of-revelation route, which focuses on the importance of the facts of the Bible, the events-of-revelation route stresses the importance of interpreted events. The contents of the Bible are not primarily a collection of facts that confirm God's truthfulness, but the record of the events through which God has acted in history. When interpreted by faith, the Bible witnesses to the story of God's salvation. God's saving acts in history provide the theme which unifies the diverse parts of the Bible.

The specific historical settings and frames of reference of the Bible are of vital importance for the events-of-revelation route. God's self-revelation did not occur in the form of some eternal truths or as some timeless universal ideal. God entered history, first in the events of the story of Israel and then preeminently in the life of Jesus Christ. Revelation is concrete historical events, rather than abstract factual statements. The people of God are redeemed by God's saving acts in history, rather than by assent to propositions about God's salvation.

Obstacles. Critics of the events-of-revelation route from Bible to doctrine especially point to its inadequacies in encompassing the entire range of Scripture.[23] Its "event theology" is seen as too limiting of the diverse ways in which Christian communities have experienced the revelation of God.

One major obstacle faced by those who defend the events-of-revelation route is its restriction of revelation to saving *acts* of God. Is revelation always limited to a public act—a historical event? Granted that public events such as the exodus and especially the crucifixion of Jesus play a central role in the Bible, are they the only kinds of revelation?

The Bible also contains stories of revelation which would seem to be more private and less like a public event. The Scriptures contain numerous stories in which God comes to persons in dreams. These stories are not just on "the fringes" of the Bible, but as Matthew's account of the angel's appearances to Joseph illustrates (1:20; 2:13, 19, 22), they are part and parcel of the gospel story (cf. also the wise men in 2:12 and Pilate's wife in 27:19).

Similarly, biblical stories abound of God's revelation coming to people in visions. Both prophets in the Old Testament and apostles in the New Testament (especially in Acts and of course Revelation) are the recipients of these visions. Although these visions have important public implications for Israel and the church, as forms of revelation they would seem to be more like private experiences than public events.

A second major obstacle encountered by those who take the events-of-revelation route is the dominance it gives to history over all other categories (genres) of literature and methods of interpretation. Although it is true that a number of the books of the Bible might be classified into a broadly conceived category of ancient historical writing, this is certainly not true of all of the books of the Bible.

The Psalms are clearly poetry, rather than history, even when they are dealing with historical subjects. In fact, scholars have great difficulty in dating the Psalms historically. One of the reasons for this may be that treating this poetry as history is putting it into a category into which it does not fit—what philosophers might label as a category mistake.

The parables of Jesus are another obvious but important example of this obstacle. These stories were never told as historical narratives (even though the occasions of their telling and retelling may be important historical events). Analyzing them using modern literary methods may yield much more helpful interpretation than the application of standard historical techniques.[24]

Defenders of the events-of-revelation route (e.g., John Baillie[25]) commonly find themselves arguing that even nonhistorical parts of the Bible can and must be treated historically, since they fit into the framework of the Bible as a historical book. This kind of argument tries to force all of the Bible into one mold—the historical one. The diversity of the Bible is sacrificed to the theological need for uniformity.

No one genre and no one discipline of interpretation can do justice to the variety of the Bible and its ongoing impact on the life of Christian communities. A multidisciplinary approach to biblical interpretation and theological reflection is needed if the journey from Bible to doctrine is to be a balanced one.

A third major obstacle faced by defenders of the events-of-revelation route is the subordination of revelation in the Bible to revelation as an event. According to the history-of-salvation view, God's primary self-revelation does not happen in Scripture but in events that happened in history, to which the Bible witnesses. These events themselves cannot be recovered. All we can do is reconstruct them from the records we have in the Bible.

Such reconstructed history is subject to all of the difficulties discussed earlier in this chapter regarding the selection and determination of historical facts. The ambiguity of relying on historical reconstruction of revelatory events should give evangelical Christians good reason to wonder whether the events-of-revelation road is the best way to make the journey from the inspired truth of the Bible to Christian doctrine.

The Doctrine of Revelation "Breakdown"
The obstacles we have discovered along both the facts-of-revelation

and the events-of-revelation routes point to a common, underlying theological problem. The problem can be located in the doctrine of revelation in Christian theology. Is the world of ambiguous historical facts and reconstructed historical events—the world "behind the text" of the Bible—the primary place where Christians should be looking when they read Scripture? How did we ever come to think that it should be? In order to respond to these questions, we need to begin with a brief overview of the modern historical turning point of the ways Christians have thought about revelation.[26]

Turning point of the doctrine. Before the eighteenth century the doctrine of revelation was not a major issue for Christian theology. Theologians believed that although people were blinded by sin from knowing God, humanity was able to come to know God through grace. Revelation was commonly understood as the communication of information about a God who could be known, however imperfectly.

Thus, Christian theologians were assuming that, by the gift of God's grace, knowledge of God was available through revelation. God might be known in a variety of ways through different kinds of revelation. One might learn of God from observing nature or from reflecting philosophically or from examining one's conscience. These sorts of ways of knowing God were classified as general revelation. Alternatively (and more importantly), one could learn of God through the special revelation given to the Christian church in the Bible. In any case, what was important was that God was able to be known.

Theologians before the eighteenth century did not think they had to prove that God was able to be known by humanity. Rather, they assumed it. The knowability of God was a *background belief*—a belief upon which many other beliefs depend and which is assumed to be so basic that it does not need explicit proof. Since it was not seen as much of a problem to believe that by God's grace humanity receives knowledge of God, the doctrine of revelation was a secondary issue for Christian theologians. The primary issue for Christian theology was not revelation, but how one was saved or transformed by God's grace.

The coming of the Enlightenment dramatically changed this situation. The turning point for the doctrine of revelation may be located in the work of Immanuel Kant (1724-1804), the philosopher whose writing marked a high point of the German Enlightenment. Kant's classic work *Critique of Pure Reason* maintained that it is impossible for us directly to know "transtemporal realities"—things that are beyond space and time. We cannot even know sensory things in themselves. Instead what we know is the way things appear to us ("phenomena"); we know things as we perceive them to be in our minds. Kant argued that our minds provide structure or prior patterning for what seem to us to be direct sensory experiences.[27]

Kant's Enlightenment philosophy shook the foundations of traditional Christian theology by challenging the background belief that God is able to be known. Although he personally believed in God, Kant rejected the many so-called philosophical proofs for God's existence. He maintained that it was impossible rationally to prove the existence of God, yet one could affirm God by faith.[28]

As a result of Kant's philosophical challenge, theologians could no longer *assume* that knowledge of God was available to humanity as a gift of God's grace. Responding to Kant's claims about the limits of rational human knowledge, theologians thought that they must show how it was plausible to believe in the availability of the knowledge of God. If they could not rationally prove that such knowledge was available, at least they wanted to show that it was reasonable for Christians to hold such a belief. Theologians felt compelled to show the rational grounds or philosophical foundations for their belief in God's grace.

Therefore the primary issue for modern theology which takes seriously the questions raised by the Enlightenment shifted. Instead of the question of salvation ("How do we know God?"), the question of the possibility of knowledge of God predominated ("How do we know that it is possible to know God?"). In more popular terms, the first question of theology changed from "How can we be saved?" to "What knowledge do we have to go on?"

This shift brought the doctrine of revelation onto center stage. No longer was revelation a secondary doctrine, based upon a background belief shared by almost everyone in Western culture. Instead, revelation became the first doctrine for theology to consider. Revelation became the subject of "theological prolegomena"—the things which need to be said before Christians can even begin to talk about the doctrine of God.

Elaborately argued doctrines of revelation may be found at the beginning of all sorts of Protestant theologies. Whether the theologian is labeled liberal (e.g., Paul Tillich, John Macquarrie) or conservative (e.g., B. B. Warfield, Carl F. H. Henry) the dominance of the doctrine of revelation is everywhere.

This Enlightenment-fueled transformation of the doctrine of revelation from a secondary doctrine waiting in the wings to the primary doctrine on center stage is a distinguishing mark of Christian theology in the modern era. Such a dramatic change has created the possibility of a serious breakdown in our journey from the Bible to Christian doctrine. For if we become ensnared in the complex philosophical tangles of the doctrine of revelation, we may never be able to move toward our destination of reflection on the great mystery of God.

Critique of the doctrine. The center-stage position of the doctrine of revelation has encouraged both Christians who follow the facts-of-revelation route and those who follow the events-of-revelation route to turn their eyes to the world "behind the text" of the Bible. The Enlightenment pressure to find "historical evidence" for the revealed truth of faith (or for the lack of faith) represents a great hazard for our journey.[29] If we make too much of a connection between the Bible and history, we will spend all our efforts trying to verify the Bible by the ambiguous and changing historical facts or events we reconstruct. If we make too little of a connection between the Bible and history, then our faith will lack relevance to everyday life and be subject to flights of fancy.[30]

The central role given to the doctrine of revelation in modern theology has pushed defenders of the facts-of-revelation and events-of-revelation routes toward making the relationship between the Bible and the historically reconstructed world behind the text too close. "History" is called on to verify or dispute the truth of theological claims in ways that are inappropriate both to the truth of Scripture and the limitations of historical knowledge. Polemical theological rhetoric and fruitless historical assertions characterize a kind of evangelical theology which is unable to maintain a balance between the theological authority of Scripture and the findings of historical research. The endless disputes among some evangelicals about the inspiration of Scripture, resulting in theories that die amidst a thousand qualifications, exemplify this loss of balance. Instead of this unbalanced relationship, the essential historical aspects of the Bible should be seen as one necessary dimension of the larger issue of the authority of Scripture for our Christian faith and practice.

The contemporary critique of the doctrine of revelation, which we will now examine, points out some serious dangers of breakdown for such revelation-centered theologies. We will examine three "trouble spots" where the breakdown can occur.

The first trouble spot is biblical. The most common biblical use of the word *revelation* is as an "uncovering" (1 Sam 3:21; 2 Sam 7:27; Dan 2:19ff; Rom 2:5; 16:25; Gal 1:12; Eph 3:3; Rev 1:1). Something that has been hidden will be revealed. As Jesus declares in Matthew 10:26, "for nothing is covered up that will not be uncovered [revealed], and nothing secret that will not become known" (cf. Lk 12:2).

Revelation is used to refer to this process of God's revealing a mystery, a prophecy, a secret to God's people. The Bible does *not* use the term as a way to describe all of God's dealings with humanity.[31] In the Bible, though revelation is important, not all of the works and ways of God are encompassed under the term.

Yet theologians who follow either the facts-of-revelation route or the events-of-revelation route use revelation as an umbrella concept. *Revelation* is the term that seeks to cover all of God's historical dealings with humanity. Under pressure from the Enlightenment question "What evidence do you have to go on?" the concept of revelation becomes inflated into a theological metaphor which embraces all of Scripture. In this view, what matters about the Bible is its status as revelation, rather than what the Bible actually says about revelation.

The treatment of revelation as an umbrella concept imposes a modern theological framework and its historical concerns upon the Bible. This broad view of revelation fails to reflect the more specialized way in which the Bible itself speaks of revelation. The Bible's authority as holy Scripture encompasses more than its important account of revelation. As a result, a revelation-centered theology is vulnerable to the charge that it is biblically inadequate.

The second trouble spot where a breakdown of the doctrine of revelation can occur is philosophical. When modern theologians write about the doctrine of revelation, they typically turn to an area of philosophy called epistemology. This branch of philosophy studies questions of how we come to know. What is the nature of knowledge and on what is it based? What are the limits of our knowledge, and how do we know it is true?

Modern theologians have relied on arguments from epistemology to show how we can know God. A doctrine of revelation that emphasizes either facts or events needs to show how one moves from those facts or events to knowing God. For example, how do the facts or events of the exodus of Israel from Egypt serve as revelation of God, rather than just as data for the history of Israel? How does God's self-revelation occur in the exodus story? How do we know that it is God who is revealed and not just some tribal deity of Israel?

In order to answer these kinds of questions, theologians who recognize Kant's limitations on sensory knowing have found themselves forced to create a special category for the knowledge of revelation.[32] Although revelation has some similarities to other knowledge we possess, it is different from the everyday knowledge we claim of facts or events. This difference lies in the quality of special knowing or "intuition" which characterizes revelation.

When the Israelites perceive God's revelation in the exodus, they encounter God's gracious presence with them, delivering them from the Egyptians. How do they know that it is *God* who delivers them, rather than simply the historical facts of Egyptian chariots stuck in the mud or the timing of some historical events? Theologians, both conservative and liberal, have relied on a special category of knowing, intuition,[33] to describe the reality of the Israelites' knowledge of God's revelation.

This special category of intuition used to explain the doctrine of revelation asserts but cannot prove philosophically the priority of God's presence. The reality of God is assumed before any strictly logical account of the facts or events of revelation. Thus, the doctrine of revelation—complete with its special category of intuition—is assumed to be a philosophical foundation for Christian theology. Much of the remaining truth of Christian doctrine then rests on the truth of this foundation.

This understanding of the doctrine of revelation is liable to philosophical breakdown on two counts. First, its special category of intuition looks like special pleading for the truth of Christianity in the court of philosophy. Such special pleading is very rarely convincing to those who are not already Christians (or who are not already predisposed to Christianity for other reasons). The special category of intuition found in doctrines of revelation seems incoherent with other forms of knowing.

The second count of the philosophical indictment is that all forms of knowing which claim to rest on universal philosophical foundations are suspect today.[34] The shift of Western culture from Enlightenment-based modernity to postmodernity means that Christian theology cannot rely on the assumption of commonly accepted philosophical foundations. If philosophers are unsure of the existence of any foundations which are rationally true for all, then to base Christian doctrine on the assertion of such a foundation seems like a philosophical dead end. Is it wise to rest the truth of Christian doctrine upon a philosophical foundation at a time when many persons no longer accept any philosophical foundations?

It seems that many modern theologians have reversed Anselm's point of view, which we discussed in the first chapter. A doctrine of revelation based on universal philosophical foundations seems to assume that understanding leads to faith, rather than that faith leads to understanding. Therefore, instead of giving the doctrine of revelation a center-stage position in theology, wouldn't it be better to begin with our basic Christian convictions and then move on to deal with the diverse ways in which we understand our knowledge of God?

Besides the biblical and philosophical trouble spots which can lead to a breakdown of the doctrine of revelation, we also must consider an important pastoral challenge to the modern emphasis on revelation. As we mentioned in our earlier discussion of the historical turning point of the doctrine, before the Enlightenment the question of being saved or transformed by God's grace was the important one for Christian theology. This emphasis was especially highlighted by the teaching of the Reformation of the sixteenth century about grace and faith.[35] Following the Enlightenment, the focus of Christian theology shifts to an emphasis on reason and evidence.

This shift has important consequences for Christian doctrine. Instead of God's saving grace serving as the most important question for theological interpretation, the doctrine of revelation itself becomes the first and often the most important question. So theologians and pastors become entangled in matters of apologetical evidence, instead of expounding saving grace. Demonstrating "the reasonableness of Christianity"[36] rather than the power of salvation dominates the ways in which Christians seek to teach the gospel in the modern world.

The implications of this shift for the pastoral needs of persons involved with the churches are serious ones. Christian theology gradually divorces itself from the day-to-day realities of salvation and the Christian life. Being saved or transformed by God's grace is seen as having little to do with sound Christian doctrine. Christians struggle to discover any connections between the revealed truths of Christian doctrine and the daily decisions of their Christian lives.

In addition, the worship life of the Christian community becomes paralyzed between the false alternatives of intellectualism (faith as assent to propositions) and subjectivism (faith as emotion divorced from reason). The old worship guideline that "the law of praying is the law of believing" *(lex orandi, lex credendi)* is abandoned. It becomes very difficult for evangelical Christians to hold together the language of a revelation-centered theology with the language of warm-hearted Christian experience.

Furthermore, the language of a biblically colored psychology gradually replaces the language of a biblically shaped theology in the practice of ministry. Christian ministers are better able to describe the psychological problems of people than to guide their spiritual growth.

Therefore the doctrine of revelation, located at center stage in Christian theology, is in serious danger of breakdown today. The biblical, philosophical and pastoral trouble spots that have emerged lead thinking Christians to question whether the road through the doctrine of revelation—by either the facts-of-revelation route or the events-of-revelation route—is the best way to go. Isn't there a better way to relate the Bible to history—a way that acknowledges but avoids being trapped by the ambiguities of reconstructing historical facts and events in the world behind the text of the Bible?

In the next chapter we will examine another route for our journey from the Bible to Christian doctrine—the road of canonical hermeneutics. Through a deeper understanding and application of the Bible as canon we may find a better guide for our theological pilgrimage.

3. Discovering a Better Route
The Bible as Canon

OUR JOURNEY FROM THE Bible to Christian doctrine is in search of a better way. The obstacles we encountered on the old roads have given us good reason to wonder whether we can find a better alternative than the facts-of-revelation and events-of-revelation routes. Each generation of Christians is called to discover, or perhaps rediscover, the paths God has provided for its theological pilgrimage. The mind's journey to God is a lifelong spiritual quest. We are commanded to love God with all of our mind, not simply to follow someone's "seven simple steps" to truth!

We will be describing in this chapter a new mode of transportation for the journey—canonical hermeneutics—which is based on an ancient idea, the concept of canon. Like most significant new directions in theology, canonical hermeneutics is not something created out of thin air, but rather is a renewed understanding and reinterpretation of how God has spoken and continues to speak to the people of God through the Scriptures.

Canonical hermeneutics seeks to avoid the dangers of breakdown to which revelation-centered theologies are exposed, which we examined at the end of the last chapter. A wholistic understanding of the Bible based on its use as Scripture substitutes for the dubious, external foundation of theologies which move revelation onto center stage. Instead of making our primary focus the facts and events in the world behind the text of Scripture, we are encouraged to focus on the canonical books themselves and our use of them as Holy Scripture. This chapter will first examine carefully the model which serves as the basis for canonical hermeneutics—the canonical approach to biblical interpretation developed by Brevard Childs. To provide sample "maps" for our journey, we will then survey some examples of Childs's canonical exegesis of specific books of the Bible. These interpretations will illustrate what his model looks like in practice. The chapter will conclude by proposing four modifications to Childs's canonical approach. These alterations seek to improve Childs's model in response to specific criticisms of its weaknesses by other biblical scholars and theologians.

The Model: Childs's Canonical Approach

Brevard S. Childs (b. 1923), a professor of Old Testament at Yale University, developed his canonical approach as an attempt to reenvision the enterprise of biblical interpretation and its connection to biblical theology. Although he was himself a skilled practitioner of historical-critical methods of biblical interpretation, Childs was dissatisfied with the results of these methods for the broader theological task of the church's interpretation of Scripture. Historical-critical methods, like form criticism and tradition criticism, provided valuable information about the background and formation of the biblical texts (the world behind the text), but offered little illumination for the challenge of interpreting the meanings of the Scripture to communities of faith.

Childs has sought to prevent the misunderstanding of his approach as simply one more historical-critical method of interpreting the Bible. Thus he avoids using terms like "canon criticism" and "canonical criticism" to describe his views, instead preferring terms like "the canonical approach" to interpretation or "exegesis in a canonical context." This broader terminology also differentiates Childs's perspective from that of other scholars[1] who have views of the authority of Scripture which are not as high as those of Childs.

In learning about Childs's canonical approach, we first will give considerable attention to the complex question of defining canon. How does Childs use the term *canon* in comparison with the views and criticisms of other scholars? Next we will turn our attention to some of the background issues which influence the theological environment in which Childs's approach develops. In particular, we will examine how the "postcritical" hermeneutics of Karl Barth assists Childs in charting his way across "the desert of criticism." Then we will look more closely at Childs's concept of the canonical shape of Scripture, which he asserts has been largely ignored by historical-critical methods of biblical interpretation. We will conclude our description of Childs's model with an analysis of its controversial emphasis on interpreting the final form of the biblical text, that form of the text which (in translation) serves as the Bible which Christians read today.

Defining canon. Childs's use of the term *canon* extends far beyond the list of sixty-six books which make up the Bible used by Protestant churches. We commonly call these books "*the* canon." They are the end result of a long historical process guided by the inspiration of God. Childs uses *canon* (without the article) to refer to the entire historical process of the formation of the Bible and its continuing authority in the life of faith communities. He uses the term *canonization* to refer to the final stages of the process of determining what will be included in the canon. Therefore, while *canon* embraces the entire process of the development and authority of the Bible, *canonization* focuses on the final boundary setting.

Canon is both a historical and a theological process. To think about the Bible as canon is to think about the authoritative role it has for communities which read it as Scripture, God's holy Word for the people of God. Of course, people—whether they are Christian or not—can read the Bible in a variety of ways. The Bible can be read as literature, as a source for archaeological information, as documents of ancient history or sources for the history of religion. Although each of these ways of reading the Bible may have a certain legitimacy, none of them represents the principal way in which Christians have read the Bible. Christian communities (and Jewish communities as well) have read the Bible as *Scripture*—God's written Word which is authoritative for their faith and practice.

The uses of the terms *Scripture* and *canon* blend together in Childs's approach. While *Scripture* encompasses more of the qualities of the Bible received in the church, *canon* points toward the authority of the Bible in the faith community. The canonical approach focuses on the historical and theological process through which Christians have come to read and interpret the Bible as Scripture.

An important consequence of a canonical reading of the Bible is that different stages of the process of the formation of Scripture do not automatically receive different theological value. This removes the illusion that an older part (or layer) of a biblical book is of more significance than a part which was added later. (Childs's canonical exegesis of Amos, which we will examine later in this chapter as one of our sample maps, provides a clear-cut example of this situation.) The fact that a passage is primary or secondary in terms of the historical process of the formation of the Bible does not mean that it is of more or less importance to the theological message of the book. Including a text in the canon means that it has theological importance for the communities who read it as Scripture.

Since both Jews and Christians read the books of the Hebrew Bible (our Old Testament) as Scripture, Childs's approach includes specific recognition of the insights into these books which God has granted to Jewish interpreters. Not only were most of the books of the Bible written by Hebrew authors for Hebrew audiences, but the ongoing Jewish community has continued to study and live by the texts of the Hebrew Bible in ways that are important for Christians to consider.

Childs's definition of *canon* is particularly in tension with the work of scholars (e.g., Albert Sundberg[2]) who want to make a sharp distinction between *Scripture* and *canon*. Such a sharp distinction separates the concept of canon from the long historical process of the formation of Scripture. According to this opposing view, *canon* should be used only to refer to a "closed collection" of scriptural texts. *Scripture* is seen as a more open and fluid category, while *canon* points to an authoritative fixed list of books. Canon is thus set apart from the historical process of the origin and development of Scripture. Instead, canon is restricted to the final boundary-setting process Childs calls canonization.

The final stages of the boundary-setting process for the canon in Judaism occur after the separation of Christianity from Judaism in the late first century. So approaches which make a sharp distinction between Scripture and canon, restricting the theological authority of canon to the later period of canonization, have the effect of claiming a complete separation between the Hebrew canon and the Christian one.[3] For both the Hebrew and Christian Bibles, the historical development of Scripture is seen as a distinct process largely isolated from the later development of the theological authority of the canon.

Those who make a sharp distinction between Scripture and canon run into historical difficulty when they encounter unexpectedly early statements of the canonical authority of biblical books. The most famous of these is the first-century claim of Josephus (c.37-c.100 C.E.) for a closed canon to the Hebrew Bible. Josephus's description of a twenty-two-book canon (*Against Apion* 1.37-43)[4] differs from the traditional Jewish counting of twenty-four books, which (by combining works) are equivalent to our thirty-nine books of the Old Testament. Yet Josephus's claim clearly challenges the notion that the historical development and the theological authority of Scripture can be neatly separated.

As we have seen, Childs's definition of canon blends the historical development and theological authority of Scripture into one complex process. The relationship between Scripture and canon, both in the early stages of the formation of the traditions of Scripture and in the later stages of the canonization of Scripture, is a continuing dynamic of interpretation in the life of communities of faith. The Christian church's receiving of the canon of Scripture is not a one-shot decision, but the culmination of God's guidance (inspiration) expressed throughout the stages of the formation and acceptance of the Bible as the authoritative Word of God.

Crossing the "desert of criticism." Paul Ricoeur's picturesque phrase "the desert of criticism"[5] portrays the terrain across which Childs's canonical approach seeks to travel. The historical-critical method of biblical interpretation, while offering some important insights about the formation of the Bible and the world behind the texts, has not fulfilled its promise for the Christian community. (In fact, many evangelicals have even developed the impression that "higher criticism" is destructive of biblical faith.) Biblical theology and the church's appropriation of the Bible have not flourished under the reign of critical, "scientific exegesis." The biblical texts have been carefully analyzed through an expanding array of new methods of criticism, but the Scripture has not often been heard speaking in new ways as the Word of God.

Even though Childs was well trained in historical-critical methods, his dissatisfaction with this theological situation led to his search for a new approach to biblical interpretation. Childs sought a perspective which would not abandon the insights of historical criticism, but would put them in the service of the larger theological task. Biblical interpretation is not ultimately a quest to amass all possible information about the historical background of the text and to offer various conflicting hypotheses regarding the history of its formation. Biblical interpretation is finally about enabling the people of God to hear the Word of God in Scripture. All of the other information gathered and theories proposed by biblical scholars are of importance to the Christian community as they deepen and illumine understanding of the ways in which God has spoken and continues to speak to the people of God through Scripture.

Childs's development of the theological perspective of his canonical approach was strongly influenced by the Protestant theologian Karl Barth (1886-1968). Childs was exposed to Barth's theology when Childs was a doctoral student studying Hebrew grammar with Walter Baumgartner in Basel, Switzerland, where Barth was teaching. But it was not until later in his career, when Childs was experiencing his dissatisfaction with the theological limitations of Old Testament historical-critical methods, that a "change of heart" about the value of Barth's approach to Scripture began to take place.[6]

Barth's theological interpretation of the Bible provides Childs with some key hermeneutical tools for developing a canonical approach to cross the desert of criticism.[7] We will briefly examine three of these in the remainder of this section: (1) Barth's focus on interpreting the text as it stands, (2) the "postcritical" perspective of Barth's hermeneutics and (3) Barth's emphasis on the theological nature of canon in interpreting Scripture.

Barth's approach to biblical interpretation is often called "theological exegesis," since its great concern is in hearing the Word of God speak through the words of the Bible. The task of interpreting the Bible as Scripture begins with the "act of observation."[8] The reader carefully and prayerfully examines the text he or she is seeking to interpret. This first phase of the process is the place where Barth locates the historical-critical interpretation of Scripture.

For Barth historical-critical studies are not an end in themselves, but rather a preliminary step in the process of theological exegesis. The usefulness of historical investigation lies not in the way it reconstructs the earlier stages of development of the texts we have in the Bible, but in the way it illuminates the texts we have in hand. Interpreting the text as it stands is the goal of the process.[9] The texts of the Bible must be allowed to speak the Word of God to us in the precise form in which the church reads and recognizes them as the Word of God. All earlier stages of the traditions of the Bible are important insofar as they help us hear the Word of God in the text as we find it in the Scripture.

Barth's focus on interpreting the text as it stands, rather than the interpretation of a critically reconstructed text behind the text in the Bible, offers a valuable key to the development of Childs's approach. This is because Barth's emphasis on the text as it stands shapes Childs's emphasis on the final form of the text. (We will examine the significance of this controversial emphasis of Childs later in my description of his approach in this chapter.) By subordinating all other stages of the historical process of the formation of the biblical texts to this focus on the text as it stands, Barth offers Childs a hermeneutical tool for successfully navigating the critical desert.

A second vital contribution which Barth's theological exegesis offers to Childs's canonical approach is a postcritical perspective. Barth does not ignore the value of the historical-critical method of interpreting the Bible. He recognizes the legitimacy of such study and seeks to incorporate its findings. The issue, however, is that the central meanings of the Scripture do not lie in the constantly changing historical world scholars reconstruct behind the text of the Bible. Rather, the text itself is the vehicle through which God has spoken and continues to speak the Word of God to the people of God.

Barth's postcritical hermeneutics seeks to give historical investigation and its critical reconstruction of the world in which the Bible was formed its rightful place, but historical-critical research marks the beginning, rather than the end, of the theological journey. First one observes the distinctions between different levels of tradition in the texts, but then one moves ahead to attempt to discover wholistic meanings in the texts as they stand. The initial historical distinctions move into the background, which informs but does not control, the ways in which God speaks through the texts today.

Barth uses his interpretation of the story in Numbers 13—14, where Moses sends the spies into the Promised Land, as an example of this dynamic process. After examining the historical-critical distinctions between elements of "history in the stricter sense" and storylike "saga" in the passage, Barth declares, "When the distinctions have been made they can be pushed again into the background and the whole can be read . . . as the totality it professes to be."[10]

Postcritical hermeneutics is suspicious of the ways in which the historical-critical method has been used to dismiss or ignore biblical interpretations which predate the rise of modern historical methods following the Enlightenment. Such traditional biblical interpretations have much to teach us about the ongoing communication between God and the people of God through Scripture. In their quest to find "the original" source of a biblical text or tradition, historical-critical methods ironically often have ignored the important history that occurs after the formation of the text.

The postcritical perspective of Barth's theological exegesis foreshadows the declining dominance of historical-critical methods of interpreting the Bible. Contemporary biblical scholars seek to use a great and sometimes confusing variety of approaches to discover the meanings of the biblical texts.[11] Barth's attempt to retain a place for historical-critical study in hermeneutics, while moving toward more inclusive theological meanings of Scripture, provides a point of view that is echoed in Childs's canonical approach.

The final hermeneutical tool which Barth's theological exegesis provides for crossing the desert of criticism is Barth's own understanding of the concept of canon. Although the idea of canon is, of course, not nearly so important and well developed in Barth's theology as it is in Childs's approach to biblical interpretation, Barth's insight into the theological nature of canon is strongly paralleled by Childs's view.

For Barth, the Bible is "self-authenticating." The Bible bears witness to itself as God's revelation. The Scripture brings its own credentials to those who read it in faith seeking understanding. Therefore, it is incorrect to think of the canon as a list of books which the church created. The canon is God's revelation, which the church *recognized* in these particular books. The church doesn't form the canon; God does. In the canon the church recognizes God's Word.[12]

Barth emphasizes the connection that the early church made between canon as a rule or standard and the "rule of truth" or rule of faith, which refers both to the formation of Scripture and to doctrinal standards that developed in the church. Canon is the rule that in these specific texts—in these particular books—the church has heard and continues to hear the Word of God.[13]

Barth rejects the idea that some parts of the Bible are more inspired or more of a part of the Word of God than others. Persons who hold this view (e.g., Martin Luther) use some other theological standard to create a "canon within the canon." For Barth, the entire canon is the written Word of God.[14] Even though the biblical text is uncertain in places and disagreement exists over the exact boundaries of the canon, Barth claims that all of this simply reflects the divine-and-human nature of Scripture as "the Word of God in the words of men."[15]

For Barth, canon is first of all a theological concept, and only secondarily a historical concept. The canon creates the context within which theological exegesis takes place. There is no neutral zone, where one can stand in scientific detachment and reconstruct the world behind the text. What we have is the canonical context of Scripture, within which the Bible is to be interpreted by and for communities of believers.

Therefore, the hermeneutics of Karl Barth forms much of the theological background on which Childs builds his canonical approach. Barth's focus on the text as it stands, his postcritical perspective on hermeneutics and his emphasis on the theological nature of canon provide important hermeneutical tools to assist Childs's canonical approach in its journey across the desert of criticism.

Discerning the canonical shape. The Bible is not a random collection of documents from ancient Israel and the earliest days of the church. The books of the Bible have definite patterns of meaning, themes, quotations, allusions, forms of organization and other connections within each book and between one another. Christians believe that although the Bible consists of many books, through the guiding hand of God's providence, it has been shaped to be read as one book. The Bible is read as a theological whole by Christians.

The process of canon has given a definite, written shape to the traditions which make up the Bible. The canonical shape reflects the ways in which Jews and Christians were led by God to fashion the elements of Scripture into a theological whole which is authoritative for the people of God. As canon the Scripture functions as a unified witness to God's ways and works.

One major way in which Christians read the Bible canonically is through reading each testament in light of the other. For example, understanding what the New Testament means when it calls Jesus "the Christ" requires an understanding of Jewish and Christian messianic readings of Old Testament texts. Further, a Christian reading of an Old Testament messianic passage requires a level of understanding that goes beyond the horizons of its original Jewish contexts to embrace the story of Jesus.

At the level of individual books of the Bible, perceptive canonical readers can discern numerous examples where a given tradition has been reshaped to speak to a new generation. We will be looking at a dramatic example of this process later in this chapter in the book of Deuteronomy. Even the Greek name of the book (*deuteros,* "second"; *nomos,* "law") reflects the pattern of canonical shaping.

The shaping of a given text to reflect its place in the larger canonical whole does not mean that there is only one final interpretation for the passage. The canonical shape of a passage works more like clues for understanding a passage, especially in light of its larger biblical contexts. Good interpreters will take account of all of these clues, but mindful that "God hath yet more light to be revealed in His Holy Word,"[16] they will avoid claiming that they have the one correct view. Thus, there is considerable room within the idea of the canonical shape of Scripture to allow for interaction between the Bible and its varied readers.[17]

Childs contends that one of the great inadequacies of historical-critical methods of interpreting the Bible is their ignoring the canonical shape of Scripture. The typical procedure of historical-critical interpretation is to seek to reconstruct the original historical setting of a text by peeling away the layers of tradition.[18] In the process of the formation of a biblical text different authors and editors, guided by the inspiration of God, have shaped the elements of the text into the final form we have as Scripture. These efforts, which give the text its canonical shape, are specifically what historical-critical interpreters are seeking to *remove* in their quest to recover the original setting of a text.

The consequences of this critical method are historical reconstructions of the Bible which in effect have "decanonized" it. The very aspects of the biblical text which have been used to enable it to speak to later generations of the people of God have been cast aside as secondary or peripheral. The text is locked into a reconstructed historical context, which seems far removed from the contemporary world of those who are seeking to read it as Scripture. The "decanonization" of Scripture by the removal of its canonical shape is somewhat analogous to the loss of an onion by peeling away its layers. In the process of the quest for the center, the onion itself is reduced to a collection of peelings!

In contrast, Childs maintains that discerning the canonical shape of biblical texts will enable Christians to make use of the valid insights of historical-critical methods, while avoiding the fragmentation that results from ignoring the ways in which the traditions of the Bible have been formed into Scripture. Merely accumulating more and more information and theories about the past does not make us better biblical interpreters. The tools of historical criticism are useful insofar as they help us understand the canonical text and wisely interpret it for our times.

This discussion of Childs's understanding of the canonical shape of Scripture and its importance for biblical interpretation has pointed to the need for a careful examination of Childs's extension of Barth's focus on the text as it stands. So this description of Childs's canonical approach will now explore his controversial emphasis on the final form of the text.

Interpreting the final form of the text. When we read the Bible as Scripture, it is through the text itself that we hear the Word of God. God speaks to the people of God in a special and authoritative way through these particular books, which constitute the canon of Scripture. Although the world behind the text of the Bible is filled with people and events who experienced God, this world is not directly accessible to us and is subject to all the ambiguities of historical reconstruction.[19]

For instance, reflecting on the experience of seeing a movie of the life of Jesus—even one supposedly based on a careful reconstruction of the events of his life—quickly uncovers some of the obvious problems. From the physical appearance of Jesus to the events leading to his crucifixion, the perspectives and prejudices of the persons making and editing the film shape what we see. We have no direct access to the ancient world in which Jesus lived. What we have access to is the Bible. It is in the text of Scripture, not behind it, that we hear the Word of God.

Guided by God's providence, the traditions of the Bible underwent a long process of shaping, as they were formed into canonical Scripture. The editors of Scripture did not seek to focus attention on their roles in canonical shaping, but instead sought to bring the canonical text itself into the spotlight. This self-obscuring role helps to account for the great difficulty scholars have in agreeing on the various stages in the formation of a canonical text. In a biblical text where editors have tried to hide rather than magnify their roles, critical attempts to disentangle and specify these roles easily degenerate into hypothetical guesswork.

The end results of the long process of canonical shaping are the final forms of the biblical books. When the Jewish and Christian communities recognized these particular books and not others as canonical, their forms no longer continued to develop, but became fixed. Although there were some differences between communities about which books—and sometimes which forms of books (e.g., Esther, Daniel)—were recognized as canonical, it is clear that a new dynamic begins to be at work. These books in their final forms were understood as part of a closed canon to be interpreted, rather than an open canon to evolve into new forms. Biblical commentary (including text-centered preaching), rather than canonical shaping, becomes the primary way in which Scripture is interpreted to meet the needs of new generations.

This new dynamic of interpreting the fixed forms of canonical Scripture to respond to the changing situations of new generations of God's people plays an important role in the lives of both Jewish and Christian communities. The Jewish development of midrash—creative homiletical explanations of and exhortations on the underlying significance of a biblical passage—reflects this dynamic of interpretation. Similarly, Christian expository preaching seeks to connect the text with the lives and issues of the people in the congregation. In both cases, a "hermeneutical circle" is established. The text of Scripture is explained in such a way as to offer an interpretation of the people's situation, while the people's changing situation is used to shed new light on the scriptural text.

Childs distinguishes the final forms of the biblical texts from all of the earlier forms of the traditions collected in the Bible for both historical and theological reasons. Historically, it is the final forms of these texts that Jews and Christians have officially recognized and read as Holy Scripture for centuries. For example, it is through the final forms of the Gospels of Matthew and Luke that Christians have heard the Word of God through Jesus' Sermon on the Mount (Mt 5:1—7:27) and Sermon on the Plain (Lk 6:17-49), rather than through a common source of the sayings of Jesus which Matthew and Luke may both have used. Theologically, it is in the final forms of the biblical texts that the people of God claim to find the authoritative witness of God. Scripture functions for evangelical Christian communities today as final authority in its final forms, not in its developing ones.

Childs understands the final form of the text to serve as the standard for interpretation. It is the beginning and ending point for all exegesis done within a canonical context. The goal of all of the various levels and stages of the text discovered by historical-critical methods is illumination of the final form of the text. If critical historical study does not help to understand the final form of the text, then it is a diversion from the purpose of a canonical interpretation of Scripture.

One important result of Childs's emphasis on the final forms of the biblical texts is a renewed connection with and appreciation for traditional ("precritical") exegesis. As I will seek to demonstrate in the next chapter, the postcritical nature of canonical hermeneutics enables us to reestablish a relationship with both the traditional and the critical phases of the history of biblical exegesis.

We have now taken a careful look at the model that serves as the basis for canonical hermeneutics—Childs's canonical approach to biblical interpretation. We have examined Childs's definition of canon, described some hermeneutical tools of Karl Barth which enable Childs to cross the desert of criticism, explored the concept of the canonical shape of Scripture and analyzed Childs's emphasis on the final form of the text. Now we are ready to inspect some biblical maps for our journey that will show us how Childs applies his model to the interpretation of specific biblical books.

The Maps: Exegesis in a Canonical Context

This detailed description of Childs's model naturally gives rise to the question of application. Before we decide to adopt Childs's canonical approach as a better way to make our journey from Bible to doctrine, we need to look carefully at some sample maps, which will show us some of the roads it proposes for interpreting Scripture. Childs's approach stresses the influence of larger contexts like biblical books and major divisions of Scripture upon biblical interpretation. So we will be surveying examples of carefully selected major themes from Childs's interpretation of three biblical books that illustrate some of the distinctives of a canonical approach.

Deuteronomy. Deuteronomy is the last book of the Pentateuch, the five books of the law of Moses (the Torah), which are central to Jewish life and worship. A canonical view sees the major problem of the book in the question of how the Mosaic law, the heart of the holy Scripture of Israel, is to be related to new generations. Childs believes that the canonical shape of Deuteronomy shows the way. The book provides "the hermeneutical key for understanding the law of Moses."[20]

The book of Deuteronomy is composed of a series of addresses delivered by Moses to the Israelites who are ready to leave the plains of Moab and enter the Promised Land. These Israelites are the new generation. (The old generation has died out in the forty years of wandering in the wilderness as a punishment for their disobedience to God.) The members of this new generation were not at Mount Sinai when Moses received the law and the Israelites experienced the ceremony of the covenant. They were not present at the events which formed Israel's religious tradition. Thus the speeches of Moses in Deuteronomy not only summarize the legal traditions of Israel but also seek to reinterpret the law for future generations.

The future-oriented application of the law by Moses applies not only to the generation which he directly addresses but to all subsequent generations of Israel. Editors of the book reshaped the legal materials in it to be more sermonic in form so that this "second law" (Deuteronomy) would address each generation of Israel who found themselves between the promise of God's election and its ultimate fulfillment. God's covenant and the legal tradition which surrounded it were not intended just for those who were with Moses at Mount Sinai, but for all of God's chosen people.

Therefore, Deuteronomy provides a dramatic example of the process of canon at work. Old traditions, in this case the Mosaic legal traditions, are brought to life for new generations. The old traditions are still authoritative for Israel, but they have been reshaped to apply to a new situation. Both the old law and the "second law" become part of the sacred Scripture. Deuteronomy shows how a canonical approach can revitalize and deepen our understanding of the function of the law of Moses in God's covenant relationship with his people Israel.

Amos. The book of Amos offers a clear illustration of the dilemma posed by historical-critical methods for thoughtful Christians who are seeking to move from Scripture to a biblically based theology.[21] The problem centers on the last chapter. Faced with the dramatic shift from complete judgment to God's promises of salvation, historical-critical interpreters have concluded that the promises of salvation (9:11-15, also possibly 9:8) were later additions to the book. In other words, the "historical Amos"—the Amos whom scholars are able to reconstruct by methods of historical-critical research—was a prophet of gloom and doom. He spoke God's message of total judgment on Israel. Later editors of the book, probably during the time of Israel's Babylonian exile, added the prophecies about God's restoration of David's kingdom (9:11-12) and the glorious age of Israel's salvation (9:13-15).

This historical-critical interpretation results in a view of the promises of salvation in Amos as "secondary." Their meaning is not central to the message of Amos but peripheral. They function something like a "P.S." added to the end of the book at a later date. Theological understandings of the book of Amos based on the "original" (i.e., the historically reconstructed) message of Amos are impoverished, rather than enriched. Instead of a prophet proclaiming both God's judgment and God's mercy, we are left with a prophet of gloom and doom.

A canonical approach to the book of Amos offers a different route of interpretation. God's promises of salvation, instead of being secondary to the meaning of the book, provide a hermeneutical key to understanding it. The book has been canonically shaped so that the messages of judgment of the historical Amos are not allowed to stand alone. Although the evidence may support a historical Amos who preached judgment only, that is not the biblical picture of Amos. Inspired by God, the biblical authors and editors gave us an Amos who proclaimed both God's judgment and God's mercy.

A canonical approach emphasizes the final form of the text as the goal of interpretation. The final form of Amos clearly includes both prophecies of judgment and prophecies of salvation. Although the canonical shaping of the book preserves the Amos who faithfully proclaims God's judgment on Israel, it places him in a larger story. The biblical theme of God's salvation of disobedient Israel guides and transforms the ways in which we are to read the prophecies of Amos. Theological understandings of Amos should be based on the final form of the entire book, not some historically reconstructed "original" text, which does not serve as Scripture for either Jewish or Christian communities. Thus, the Amos we find in Scripture—the canonical Amos—is not just a prophet of doom, but a prophet who faithfully proclaims God's judgment and witnesses to God's salvation.

Our first two sample maps have taken us through some of the territory of the Old Testament, where Childs first developed his canonical approach.[22] We have looked specifically at a book of the law (Deuteronomy) and one of the prophets (Amos). As a Christian biblical interpreter, Childs extended his approach to include the New Testament in *The New Testament as Canon: An Introduction*.[23] So our final sample map will survey some themes from Childs's exegesis of the book of Ephesians.[24]

Ephesians. Readers of the letter to the Ephesians are struck with the strongly theological nature of this epistle. Much of this theological language comes from early Christian worship and hymns. The nature and mission of the church are at the center of the message of the book.

Historical-critical interpretation, however, has not focused on this theological theme. Instead it has been preoccupied with questions of the recipients, the authorship and the form of the letter.

The absence of the words "in Ephesus" from the first verse in many of the oldest Greek manuscripts has generated much discussion, many proposals (e.g., a circular letter) and few definite conclusions about the group to whom the epistle was originally addressed. Rather than focusing on the quest for "the original addressee," Childs's canonical approach simply acknowledges that the earliest texts of Ephesians which we possess were already part of the canonical process. Regardless of when the words "in Ephesus" were included, they have the role of directing our attention to the new generation of Ephesian Christians. Although Paul knew the original church at Ephesus very well (e.g., Acts 20:17-38), his statement "I have heard of your faith in the Lord Jesus" (1:15) reveals that he knows the new generation only from a distance. The canonical function of the letter's being addressed to the Ephesians is not to send us off on a speculative search for the original addressee, but to focus our attention on how the epistle is shaped to transmit the faith to a new generation of believers.

For the past two centuries incredible amounts of scholarly attention have been devoted to the debate over the authorship of Ephesians. Was the letter written by Paul or by a later follower of Paul? Biblical scholars, both liberal and conservative, have written as if this were the most important issue in understanding the book of Ephesians. It seems as if many scholars think the book will lose its truth if they cannot historically demonstrate (or historically disprove) that Paul was the author.

Childs points out that the "historical Paul" has been made the subject of endless reconstruction, while the "canonical Paul" has been ignored. This debate does not reflect the way in which the New Testament approaches the issue. Ephesians is already included in the canon of Pauline letters in the New Testament. Therefore, the approach of first critically reconstructing a life of the historical Paul and then using it to see whether Ephesians should be included as Paul's "authentic" theology has turned things upside down. A canonical approach instead seeks to determine what effect the inclusion of

Ephesians has on the witness of the Pauline books of the New Testament. So the primary question for biblical interpretation of Ephesians should not be "Did Paul really write the epistle?" but "What role does Ephesians play in shaping the truth of Paul's witness to the gospel?"

Besides the questions of the recipients and authorship of Ephesians, scholars have devoted much energy to debating the form of the epistle. They assume that if we can decide into precisely what category of literature Ephesians falls, then we can progress toward determining its purpose. Was Ephesians originally written as an "occasional letter" or as a "theological tractate"?

Childs's canonical approach maintains that it is not the original form of the letter but its *use* by the community of faith that is most important. The sharp distinctions between occasional letter and theological tractate are blurred in the canonical shaping of the book. If Ephesians is to serve as a true witness to Paul's theology, then it must be grounded in the worship and mission of the church. The languages of gospel proclamation (theological tractate) and daily living (occasional letter) must be blended together to produce an adequate witness to God's message through Paul.

Our inspection of these sample maps of Deuteronomy, Amos and Ephesians has provided us with some concrete illustrations of how the model of Childs's canonical approach actually works in the concrete tasks of interpreting the Bible. Now having surveyed our model and examined some maps, we are ready to consider some modifications.

The Modifications: Alterations to Childs's Approach

Before we are ready to take canonical hermeneutics further along the road to Christian doctrine, we need to make some changes to the model on which it is based. Childs's canonical approach to biblical interpretation has received international response and much critical discussion among biblical scholars. Among the numerous criticisms, there are four which are of special importance. They concern (1) defining the boundaries of the canon, (2) broadening the hermeneutics of tradition, (3) describing the place of canon in the reading process and (4) including new methods of biblical interpretation. These criticisms seem to have validity, and they involve some alterations (at times rather technical) to the model itself. Taking them one at a time, we will first seek to understand and analyze the criticism, and then we will examine the modifications being proposed.

The boundaries of the canon. All Christian Bibles do not have just sixty-six books. While there is somewhat consistent agreement on the twenty-seven books of the New Testament, many Christian groups recognize additional books (and additions to books) beyond the thirty-nine books which constitute the Protestant Old Testament canon.[25] Though differently ordered and numbered, these thirty-nine books are the same in content as the twenty-four books of the Hebrew Scriptures.

Roman Catholic, Greek and Slavonic (Russian Orthodox) Bibles contain a number of additional books, as well as additions to Esther and Daniel, which they call deuterocanonical books. The Greek and Slavonic Bibles also recognize some additional writings as deuterocanonical which are not recognized in the Roman Catholic canon. Groups commonly label books "apocryphal" which they do not recognize as canonical or deuterocanonical.

Dealing with these diverse boundaries of the canon raises important concerns for Childs's approach. Childs argues that the Christian Old Testament should observe the limits of the Hebrew Scriptures. He claims that the Old Testament canon is linked to the authority of the Hebrew text, especially the Masoretic text (the standard Hebrew text used today, which was edited in the early Middle Ages). Besides the technical challenges to his exclusive choice of the Masoretic text,[26] Childs's argument fails to account for the use of the longer canon of the Greek Old Testament by the early church. The Bible of the earliest Christians was the Greek Septuagint (which included deuterocanonical books). Later the emerging Greek New Testament was added to the Septuagint. As the Vulgate and other Latin Bibles also included deuterocanonical books, it was not until the time of the Reformation that some Christians in the West (Protestants) eliminated these books from their Old Testament to follow the narrower Jewish canon.

Since a canonical approach focuses on the use of the Bible as Scripture, Childs's approach would benefit from a less rigid view of the exact boundaries of the canon. One way to picture this is to think of the canon as having a firm center and blurred edges. Most of the books are fixed around the center, but some of the books on the margins have been and are still being debated. Some Christians think these books are of secondary status (*deutero*canonical); others think they are merely apocryphal. As different groups of Christians have claimed to hear the Word of God through these books, a canonical approach could seek to evaluate critically these claims by comparing them with all of the books recognized universally by the churches and by examining their usefulness in the life of Christian communities.

The hermeneutics of tradition. Our second modification to Childs's canonical approach relates to his concept of tradition. Christians use the word *tradition* in many divergent ways. For some it represents the static burden of the past—"the dead weight of tradition." For others it points to a source of identity—"my religious tradition." Although some Christians try to maintain a complete separation between the Bible and tradition, many see the Bible as made up of truth contained in living, God-breathed tradition.

Childs's understanding of tradition and the Bible was formed by his training as an Old Testament scholar and his earliest writings, which interpreted the Bible using historical-critical methods, especially a method known as tradition history. This view focuses on the traditions behind the text of the Bible. The interpreter sifts through the layers of tradition and seeks to reconstruct critically the original traditions and the history of their development. Thus, the emphasis in this understanding of tradition falls on the *prehistory* of the biblical text—analyzing the traditions before they are formed into their fixed shape in the Bible.

Although Childs's canonical approach stresses the importance of the final form of the text for biblical interpretation, his view of tradition is still mainly preoccupied with examining matters behind the text. Detailed analyses of the historical-critical debates not only set the stage for his canonical proposals but often tend to dominate the discussion. Instead of serving as a preliminary step in the long process of interpretation, the reconstruction of the prehistory of the text consumes much of Childs's attention and energy. The historical-critical view of tradition has become a burden, rather than a legacy.

How can Childs's concept of tradition overcome the limitations of historical-critical methods which bind it to the prehistory of the text? One promising alternative is offered by the hermeneutics of the

German philosopher Hans-Georg Gadamer.[27] Gadamer's understanding of tradition is broader than Childs's. Tradition, in Gadamer's view, is a continuing conversation which embraces the entire history of the text across generations of readers. The effects which a text produces in different time periods upon various kinds of readers are all part of the tradition which shapes its meaning.

Since the Bible is a text that has spoken and continues to speak across the ages, Gadamer's model of how classic texts operate should help us to understand better the meaning of Scripture.[28] Each generation of readers, based on its own presuppositions, brings its own perspectives or points of view—its horizon—to the interpretation of a classic text. In the case of the Bible, horizons beginning with the traditions of ancient Israel and including the traditions of Christian groups today are all part of the process of shaping its significance. Meaning occurs when there is a "fusion of horizons."

For example, a contemporary understanding of the commandment to keep the sabbath, a tradition of ancient Israel which speaks to Christians today, includes the interpretive horizons of the early church (sabbath as Sunday) and the Puritans (strict community-wide moral restrictions). Each interpretive horizon (including our own present horizon) has its effects on the meaning of the text in our time. These various horizons are joined together (fused) to create the living tradition through which God speaks to the people of God.

Modifying Childs's concept of tradition to include aspects of Gadamer's broader hermeneutical view[29] would reduce Childs's preoccupation with the prehistory of the text. The historical reconstruction of the traditions which formed the Scripture would remain an important but now subordinate task. The hermeneutical question of how these texts were used as the living tradition of Scripture—how God has spoken through these specific texts to communities of Jews and Christians throughout the history of their interpretation—becomes the crucial one. Adopting this broader hermeneutical view of tradition would enable Childs's canonical approach to embrace more effectively the entire history of the interpretation of the Bible as Scripture.

The reading process. The third modification of the model of Childs's canonical approach responds to the many criticisms of his establishing a special canonical level for reading the Bible. Scholars who raise this issue commonly label it as the question of "canonical intentionality." Instead of focusing on the (often futile) attempts to use historical-critical methods to recover the historical intentions of the authors and editors of the Bible, Childs wants to recover the canonical intention of the Scripture and use it as a standard for interpretation. Yet he fails to be very clear about how this works in the reading process. How is this idea of canonical intentionality related to the ways in which communities of faith read the Bible as Scripture?

The French philosopher Paul Ricoeur[30] has developed a theory of reading which can help to clarify Childs's unclear idea of canonical intentionality. Ricoeur's theory provides a place to locate Childs's special canonical level of reading within a wider spectrum of levels of meaning.

To understand Ricoeur's theory, one must grasp the concept of the text as a "work." Although an author creates a literary text, once it has been written, it takes on a life of its own. No matter what the author intended, he or she cannot control the meaning(s) which readers give to the work.[31] The intention of the author has been "distanced" from the meanings of his or her work. The ways in which a text is structured or configured shape the meanings which the reader discerns. It is like the text now has its own intention, historically tied to but remaining separate from the author's intention. Thus, we can speak metaphorically of "textual intentionality."

Ricoeur's theory shows how different levels of language (moving from word to sentence to discourse) shape different levels of meaning. To take an oversimplified example, we can reflect on the changing levels of meaning of the word *shepherd* in the famous Twenty-third Psalm. Standing alone, the word refers to a human occupation common in ancient Israel. At the metaphorical level (the level of the sentence), we observe in the context of "The LORD is my shepherd" that *shepherd* refers to a divine occupation, no longer just a human one. This shift of meaning is confirmed by the parallelism of the remainder of the verse, "I shall not want." At a very broad level which interprets the Old Testament in light of the New (a level of discourse), Christians commonly interpret *shepherd* in relation to Jesus, "the good shepherd" of John 10:11. This level of meaning is especially attractive to Christian interpreters because of the imagery of "the darkest valley" (or "the valley of the shadow of death") in verse 4 of the psalm.

As we have seen, Childs's canonical exegesis moves in similar fashion from investigating smaller contexts (e.g., linguistic investigation of the uses of a word in a text) to larger ones (e.g., the context of the entire Christian canon). Ricoeur's theory provides a way to account for the levels of meaning accompanying various contexts of interpretation.

Ricoeur's account of the reading process enables us to understand canonical intentionality as textual intentionality based on the larger configuration of the biblical texts as Scripture. The shape of the texts themselves—what Childs calls their canonical shape—is the basis for this special level of intentionality. Canonical intentionality does not refer to the intentions of some author or editor of the books of the Bible. Rather, canonical intentionality points to the theologically authoritative shape of Scripture through which God has spoken and continues to speak to the lives of those who listen to the Word of God.

The new methods. Our final modification to the model of Childs's canonical approach relates to the inclusion of new sociological and literary methods of interpreting the Bible.[32] Childs is heavily engaged with tradition history and other methods of historical-critical exegesis but pays relatively little attention to recent sociological[33] and literary-critical approaches.[34] Such methods of interpretation when applied to the Bible seek to understand the sociocultural forces that influenced the formation and interpretation of the Scriptures and the ways in which the literary shapes of the biblical texts create different worlds of meaning for their readers.

Part of the reason for Childs's neglect of these new approaches may of course lie in Childs's own professional training and early research using historical-critical approaches to the Old Testament. There seems, however, to be a deeper theological reason that accounts for much of Childs's reluctance to support these new methods.

Childs is wary that much of the theology that underlies these new methods fails to emphasize the central role of Christ throughout the Christian canon. Instead, perspectives deriving from politics, social psychology, human development and other human centers of value are really exercising a controlling influence. Childs fears that these new directions will lead to a human-centered (anthropocentric), rather than

Christ-centered (christocentric), understanding of the Scripture.[35]

Childs's suspicions are certainly not without historical grounds. As liberal Protestant theology of the nineteenth century shows, when this focus on the human subject is combined with a belief in absolute human knowledge, atheism (e.g., Ludwig Feuerbach[36]) is not far away.

Is there a way for Childs to avoid this dangerous path while remaining open to the valuable insights into Scripture offered by the new methods of interpretation? One possibility lies in the critique of absolute human knowledge offered by Ricoeur's "hermeneutics of testimony."[37]

Ricoeur argues that the claims of the German philosopher G. W. F. Hegel (1770-1831) for absolute human knowledge should be rejected.[38] Hegel developed a philosophy of consciousness that glorified the human subject. The will progressed through culture and culminated in "absolute knowledge." In Hegel's system all of the diverse richness of historical meaning was in the end reduced to "the logic of the concept."[39] Therefore, Ricoeur declares that for Hegel "the hermeneutics of testimony is swallowed up in absolute knowledge."[40] Rejecting the assumption of absolute human knowledge, we should begin from the perspective that, like testimony, all our knowledge is only partial. As Paul declared centuries before, "For we know only in part" (1 Cor 13:9).

If Childs were to adopt Ricoeur's hermeneutics of testimony, Childs could preserve the Bible's emphasis on the importance of human witness to God's truth, while avoiding the danger of a human-centered theology that elevates human knowing to the place of God. As a result, a modified version of canonical hermeneutics can show greater openness to the contributions of recent sociological and literary methods for interpreting the Bible[41] without fear of reducing its own approach to the Bible to a human-centered perspective. Instead, a Christ-centered canonical approach to Scripture welcomes truth from any source, convinced that all truth points us toward the Truth, Jesus Christ the Lord.

The four modifications which we have examined seek to broaden and clarify Childs's canonical approach in response to significant criticisms it has received. With these alterations to our model, canonical hermeneutics can serve as an effective mode of transportation for our journey from the Bible to doctrine.

Our search for a route for the journey that is better than seeking facts or events of revelation behind the text of the Bible has led us to look at the texts of Scripture themselves. As canon these texts have been shaped, under God's guidance, to serve as authoritative Scripture for the people of God. Their authority lies in what God has used them to do—speak the Word of God to communities of believers.

Now that we have carefully examined our model of Childs's canonical approach to biblical interpretation, inspected some sample maps and made the necessary modifications, we are ready to use canonical hermeneutics to explore the surroundings.

4. Exploring the Surroundings
A Canonical Approach to Interpretation

T HE COUNTRY THROUGH WHICH we are passing in our pilgrimage from Bible to doctrine is known for its difficulty. There are numerous rugged ascents and "slippery" spots, where our journey might become sidetracked or delayed. Along the way, however, we will also glimpse some striking scenery. Our mode of transportation, canonical hermeneutics, will provide us with some new perspectives to understand and find a way through the challenging terrain.

This chapter will attempt to show how a canonical approach to biblical interpretation can strengthen our doctrine of Scripture. Canonical hermeneutics offers a way to encompass traditional interpretation and historical-critical interpretation in a larger *postcritical* theological vision. The postcritical perspective of canonical hermeneutics incorporates insights from both traditional and historical-critical exegesis into a larger theological framework. The many ways in which the Bible speaks to the people of God can be recognized and heard in an evangelical theology which emphasizes the authority of Scripture.

We will begin our explorations by examining the road markers of biblical authority. Specifically, we will consider how Scripture marks the way to right doctrine and how the concept of canon points us to the authority and boundaries of Scripture. Next the buried treasures of traditional biblical interpretation will be the subject of our quest. We will search for means to unearth these important treasures of the past in forms that are helpful to Christians today. Then our attention will turn to the excavations of historical-critical interpretation of the Bible. We will investigate some new ways of preserving the insights into the Bible offered by historical-critical methods of study, while avoiding the dangers of reducing Scripture to the sole status of an object for historical reconstruction. Finally, the chapter will close with a brief tour of the flowering gardens of postcritical interpretation. Deepening our understanding of the purposes and patterns of Scripture will serve as the focus for our development of postcritical biblical interpretation.

The Road Markers: Biblical Authority

The authority of the Bible is a belief that Christians hold dear. Evangelical Christians are especially characterized by a strong emphasis on biblical authority. When we are asked, however, to define specifically what we mean by this belief, we may resort to apologetic arguments defending the inspiration of the authors of the Bible,[1] but all too often we are reduced to slogans. "The Bible says it. I believe it. That settles it!" While such slogans may have great rhetorical impact on our emotions, they do not help us to grow in our ability to understand our faith.

Clarifying what we mean by the authority of the Bible is a vitally important—and often highly controversial—challenge for Christians today. Canonical hermeneutics can help us with this issue. A canonical perspective on biblical authority focuses on the question of how the Bible *functions* as authority for Christians. Understanding the authority of the Bible means understanding its *use*. It is not enough to declare what we as Christians believe the Bible is—stating and qualifying the various descriptions (e.g., Word of God, holy, infallible, inerrant, historically accurate, true) and then arguing over which is best. Instead, a more fruitful approach is to describe how the Bible functions authoritatively in Christian lives and communities.

Two key concepts serve as road markers in our quest for a deeper understanding of the authority of the Bible. The first concept is

"Scripture," which describes how the Bible is recognized and used as sacred writings by communities of faith. The second concept is "canon," which (as we discussed in chapter three) describes the long process of formation and the continuing authority of the particular writings which communities of Jews and Christians recognize as Scripture.

Scripture as the norm of doctrine. The teachings of the Christian faith—its doctrines—were formulated over a period of time. When Christ ascended into heaven, he left his followers with a Great Commission (Mt 28:19-20), not with a completely developed theology. As early Christians sought to carry the Christian message to the ancient world, they discovered the need to organize and express consistently their beliefs in more detail. Pagan philosophers such as Celsus[2] and Porphyry[3] challenged Christians to defend their faith by argument. In their debate with paganism, early Christian thinkers embodied the words of 1 Peter 3:15, "Always be ready to make your defense to anyone who demands from you an accounting for the hope that is in you."

Christian doctrine not only took shape in debate with the external challenges from paganism and other religious groups. It also responded to internal struggles among various groups who claimed to be Christian. An example of this process of doctrinal development may be found in the doctrine of the Trinity. Although early Christians worshiped Christ as God, the full implications of this worship for their understanding of God were only gradually worked out until they culminated in the doctrine of the Trinity in the fourth century. Christians needed to find a satisfactory way to hold together their belief in the oneness of God (monotheism) with their experience of the threeness of God (Father, Son, Holy Spirit). Through much controversy, the doctrine of the Trinity developed over these centuries to provide a way for Christians to affirm their insights into both the unity of God and the threefold nature of God. In the next chapter we will be exploring the development of this doctrine in much greater detail.

Early Christians struggled with many diverse groups (e.g., Gnostics elaborating a complex mythological view of creation and salvation) who claimed that their teachings were part of the true Christian faith. Through these controversies, which resulted in winners who understood themselves to be orthodox and losers who were labeled heretics, the early church came to see the need for a norm or "rule of faith" (Latin, *regula fidei*). The rule of faith provided a standard against which to test the contradictory claims of various groups.

Although a variety of summaries of the faith in the forms of confessions and creeds were used, gradually (as the process of forming the canon nears an end) the Scriptures themselves as a whole come to be identified as the rule of faith. The Scriptures are understood as the source of the teachings of the faith. Everything necessary to know about Christian faith and practice is contained in the Scriptures.[4] They are the norm against which all the other norms are tested. Therefore, as the rule of theology, Scripture sets the boundaries for correct doctrine.

Unfortunately, frequently in the history of Christianity the reverse has proven to be the case. Instead of Scripture functioning as the rule of doctrine, exaggerations of particular doctrines have sought to become the rule of Scripture. Proponents of a specific view have sought to read their particular opinions into Scripture (eisegesis) rather than letting the Scripture rule their view. Prooftexts have been claimed for an amazing variety of additions to and aberrations of the Christian tradition (e.g., relics, witch burnings, dated predictions of the end of the world, strategies for financial success).

An approach to theology which uses canonical hermeneutics helps us to see how many of these exaggerated elaborations and accretions to Christianity lack substantial basis in Scripture. Since Scripture is the norm of Christian doctrine, teachings or practices that are based on forced or contrived interpretation have little or no claim to be regarded as authoritative. Christians who seek to claim authority for beliefs and actions supported by such scriptural pretexts are making maps where there is no biblical territory.

In summary, Scripture serves as a road marker for biblical authority by serving as the source and standard for teaching about the faith. The norm of Scripture sets boundaries for the development and testing of Christian doctrine.

Canon as the rule of Scripture. The word *canon* was originally used by ancient Greek writers to refer to a straight rod. Later this word was used in Greek to describe a standard or rule, as Paul does in Galatians

6:16: "As for those who will follow this rule [canon]—peace be upon them, and mercy, and upon the Israel of God."[5]

The famous Jewish philosopher and biblical interpreter Philo of Alexandria (c. 20 B.C.E.-c. 50 C.E.) used the term *canon* to refer to the rule of truth.[6] This usage was adopted and extended by Christian writers who understood themselves as defenders of the faith. *Canon* came to refer to God's revealed truth. Gradually, through its association with the rule of faith, the term was identified with the developing authoritative collections of Jewish and Christian Scriptures.

Canon thus signifies the rule that these specific books, rather than other alternatives, are the ones to be read as holy Scripture. In other words, canon is the rule of Scripture.

Upon what is this rule called canon based? From the side of God *(coram Deo)* the canon reflects the affirmation that God has freely chosen to speak the Word of God to his people through these particular books which are uniquely authoritative. From the side of humanity *(coram humanibus)* the canon reflects the use that the people of God have made of these books. It is through these particular books that Christians hear the Word of God. Christians recognize these specific books as the canon of Scripture because they have heard and continue to hear God speaking to them through the reading of these works.

Therefore, on the one hand, the canon is constituted by God's speaking. On the other hand, the canon is constituted by God's people learning to hear God speaking. The church discovers the Word of God in the canon; the church does not create the canon. Yet the preservation of these sacred books by communities of faith is the means by which they are available to us today.

The church's use of canon as the rule of Scripture can be divided into two periods.[7] The first period consists of the formation of Scripture. The long process of the writing and collecting of the texts, their theological shaping and their compilation into the final forms of the Bible which we use today occurs during this period. The second period consists of the continuing theological interpretation of the Bible as Scripture by communities of faith. This long history of reading the Bible in its final forms as the authoritative Word of God begins at the end of the first period (canonization) and continues into the present.

Because of the limited historical evidence we have regarding the precise process of the formation of each of the books and larger sections of the Bible, the specific details of when the first period slides into the second are often obscure. Nevertheless, it is clear that communities of faith move from (1) theologically shaping the traditions of the Bible into their final forms as Scripture to (2) the theological interpretation of the final forms of the Bible as Scripture. For example, (1) early Christians first read, circulated and collected Paul's epistles as letters before they were recognized as canonical; then (2) later Christians read and interpreted these letters as books of the New Testament. In other words, in their history God's people have moved from the authority of canon in the process of formation to the authority of the canon in the Bibles we have today.

In summary, canon serves as a road marker of biblical authority by serving as the rule of Scripture. Canon both reflects the theological shaping of Scripture and sets the boundaries for the interpretation of Scripture as the Word of God by communities of faith.

The Buried Treasures: Traditional Interpretation

Having examined Scripture and canon as the road markers of biblical authority, we can now begin to investigate directly our surroundings in this world of theological interpretation. We are moving from exploring the "signs" which guide our journey to examining the territory itself. The first thing we notice is that "the dust of history" lies thick all around us. There appear to be an amazing number of artifacts buried in the ground, but they seem to have been neglected—abandoned for several centuries. The only explanation we see is a faded marker, which declares "Warning: Precritical Interpretation."

Stopping a passerby who turns out to be a historian, we ask about the buried artifacts and are informed that they were left behind by the Enlightenment, which has been conducting its own biblical excavations elsewhere. Our wise passerby gives a wry smile and then remarks, "Some people believe that hidden amid all those cast-off artifacts are some buried treasures."[8]

In this section we will consider how canonical hermeneutics can enable us to rediscover some of the treasures buried in the traditional biblical interpretation of the past. Instead of using the condescending term *precritical,* I will use the term *traditional interpretation,* which is both more descriptive and less pejorative of these earlier methods of interpreting Scripture. Our explorations will focus in two areas: (1) how the past division between Scripture and tradition may be reframed to be more inclusive of the living connections between the Bible and communities of faith, and (2) how the tradition of typological interpretation of Scripture may be rehabilitated to serve in our postcritical age.

Reframing tradition. Evangelical Christians, believers in Jesus Christ who hold to the primary and final authority of Scripture for Christian faith and practice, have inherited a largely negative view of tradition. Human traditions are viewed as those customs, beliefs and practices that people have tried to add to the teachings of the Bible. Such traditions are seen as possessing no authority over Christians, who instead are called to hold fast to the sole authority of Scripture.

We have received this negative view of tradition as part of our Protestant legacy from the Reformation of the sixteenth century. As Christians in the West divided into Catholic and Protestant camps, Protestants adopted the slogan of "Scripture alone" *(sola Scriptura)* in opposition to the Catholic view of "Scripture and tradition." Of course, Protestants actually developed and tenaciously clung to their own traditions (including the tradition of *sola Scriptura!*), while many Catholics would admit to the primacy of Scripture as the "rule-making rule" *(norma normans)* of all the other traditions of the church. As is unfortunately customary in fights between Christians, theological polemics made sharp, simple distinctions between the beliefs of opposing groups so that theological slogans could reinforce group identity and serve as a political rallying cry against the enemy. Protestants saw Catholics as not really believing in the authority of the Bible, while Catholics saw Protestants as rejecting the biblical and apostolic traditions of the church.

Canonical hermeneutics offers us a way to get beyond our largely negative view of tradition, while still holding to the authority of Scripture. As evangelical Christians, we need to reframe our understanding of tradition by examining the ways in which early Christians understood the relationship between tradition and the authority of Scripture. It is not that tradition gives us another source of authority besides Scripture. (That two-source theory is the old polemical Catholic view, soundly rejected by Protestants.) Rather, tradition provides the context within which the Bible is to be interpreted as Scripture.

We cannot understand the ways in which Christians in the early church interpreted the Bible unless we develop some picture of the roles that tradition played in the process. At this point Eastern Orthodox Christians, whose wholistic view of Scripture and tradition has not suffered from the polemical split which afflicts Western Christians, have much to teach us. In Eastern Orthodoxy, tradition is understood as a living reality illumined by the presence of the Holy Spirit. Tradition does not add anything to the truth found in the Scripture, but instead shapes the context of Christian community and provides a hermeneutical principle for interpreting the Bible as God's truth.[9]

So, applying this wholistic view to canonical hermeneutics, if we are trying to understand a Pauline epistle, we would not be preoccupied with the task of seeking to discern Paul's intentions when he wrote this letter. Attempting to discover the "original intention of the author" is far different from interpreting the letter in the communal contexts in which it has been received, read and preserved. (Also, the historical-critical questions about whether Paul himself actually wrote this letter would not be the focus of concern.) The key issue instead would be trying to interpret this Pauline letter itself in its context in the Christian canon. The Christian community has already heard the Word of God in this letter, recognized it as Scripture and assigned it to a specific place within the living tradition.

Therefore, although traditional biblical interpretation is unaware of later historical-critical insights and issues concerning Paul and the epistles attributed to him, it still has much to teach us about the meaning and significance of these letters as part of the living Christian tradition. Interpreting the Bible within its canonical context provides a perspective for transforming our largely negative view of tradition into a Spirit-filled, wholistic understanding.

Rehabilitating typology. One of the major reasons that historical-critical scholars of the Bible have abandoned traditional interpretation to the dustbin of history is its loss of hermeneutical control. When we read the commentaries and sermons of ancient and medieval Christian writers, forced doctrinal applications and flights of fancy abound. (Of course, the past has no monopoly on interpretation gone out of control.

Similar problems may be found in popular expositions of the Bible and in sermons today.)

At the root of this problem in traditional biblical interpretation are the methods being used. In particular, the methods of allegory and typology are subject to this loss of hermeneutical control.[10]

Allegory seeks to make a connection between someone or something (or a group of persons or things) in the text and another person or thing (or group). The latter represents the former or tells what it really means. So, for example, the explanation of the parable of the wheat and tares in Matthew 13:36-43 is an elaborate allegory:

> The one who sows the good seed is the Son of Man; the field is the world, and the good seed are the children of the kingdom; the weeds are the children of the evil one, and the enemy who sowed them is the devil; the harvest is the end of the age, and the reapers are angels. (Mt 13:37-39)

Typology is the interpretation of a person or event as representing or fulfilling a "similar situation" in the text. In contrast to allegory, typology assumes some sort of historical connection between the two parts of the correspondence. One of the most famous examples of typology is that between Christ and Adam, which Paul describes in Romans 5:12-21. In verse 14 of this passage Adam is specifically described as "a type of the one who was to come [Christ]."

Origen, the great master of allegory in the second and third centuries, dramatically illustrates the problem of losing hermeneutical control. In his *Homilies on Leviticus,* Origen extends his allegorical interpretation so far as to argue that the kidneys of the sacrificial calf represent the soul of Christ![11]

Until the Reformation of the sixteenth century the allegorical method was the dominant way Christians interpreted the Bible. A complex system of levels of meaning developed, which was rejected by many of the Reformers (e.g., Luther, Zwingli, Calvin, Melanchthon) because of its abuses. They favored instead a simpler method tied to the literal sense of Scripture.[12]

The objection that, using the allegorical method, interpreters could and did manipulate Scripture to mean whatever they wished represents a valid and continuing concern. Although a more literal interpretation certainly does not rule out the abuse of Scripture (e.g., the Salem witch trials were based on literal exegesis), the loss of hermeneutical control in the allegorical method renders it unsuitable as the primary method for studying the Bible today.

In contrast, typology offers a more controlled traditional method of biblical interpretation. Its approach of seeking a similar situation between the type (e.g., Adam) and the antitype to which it refers (e.g., Christ) and its emphasis on seeking a historical connection between elements of the correspondence provide greater hermeneutical control than is possible with allegory. Furthermore, the powerful biblical theme of prophecy and fulfillment fits together effectively with the typological method. The ties between the initial prophecy (e.g., the sign of Immanuel in Isaiah 7:14) and the events or persons that are understood as its fulfillment (e.g., the birth of Jesus in Matthew 1:22-23) may be understood as illustrations of the correspondence between type and antitype.

In the second chapter I discussed the weaknesses of a theology centered on the search for the events of revelation behind the text of the Bible. Canonical hermeneutics seeks to modify the method of typology to respond to these weaknesses, which attempt to locate the authority of Scripture outside the biblical text. The language of the Bible is the vehicle that guides the interpretation of Scripture—including typological interpretation. The goal of typological interpretation is not the description of some correspondence between events or persons in a history of salvation or special sphere of revelation outside the Bible. Rather, it is the canonical texts themselves which witness to the past, speak God's Word in the present and lead the people of God toward the future. Typological interpretation takes place within the boundaries of the canon of Scripture.

Typological interpretation within the context of the canon provides a way for Christians today to reestablish ties with traditional biblical interpretation. Through reframing tradition and rehabilitating typology canonical hermeneutics will enable us to unearth much of the buried treasure that lies abandoned under the faded warning sign of "precritical interpretation."

The Excavations: Historical-Critical Interpretation
Now that we have discussed some ways to unearth the buried treasure

of traditional biblical interpretation, the time has come to explore the biblical excavations which were moved elsewhere. As the historian we met earlier informed us,[13] during the European Enlightenment of the eighteenth century, biblical scholars started to develop new critical approaches to the interpretation of the Bible.

These approaches seek to reconstruct the history that lies behind the text of the Bible. Scholars, in their quest for the original events or traditions which gave rise to the text, attempt to identify and then strip off the various layers of tradition and editing which shaped the biblical text we have today. Material which is thought to have been added later in the history of the formation of the passage is labeled as secondary and seen as of lesser importance than the original parts of the text. The image of peeling off the husks in the search for the historical kernel of the text was frequently used by previous generations of scholars to picture this historical-critical process of interpretation.[14]

Our exploration of these historical-critical excavations will focus on two themes. First, we will examine the problem of overidentifying the Bible with history. We will investigate some of the serious consequences of this kind of historicism. Second, we will consider how canonical hermeneutics can help us to use the insights into the formation of the Bible which historical-critical interpretation provides, without falling into the danger of historicism. A *postcritical* view of historical-critical interpretation—a view that goes beyond the limits of modern, critical study based on the Enlightenment—provides a perspective for incorporating the gains of historical criticism without succumbing to its liabilities.

Rejecting historicism. Historical-critical interpretation of the Bible can easily lead us to the inadequate view that the only thing which really matters about the Bible is the history that lies behind it. The Bible is then primarily seen as a history book or, more accurately, a source for historical reconstruction. Everything else about the reading of the Bible is viewed as secondary to this overriding concern for its historical value.

The result of this view is that the contents of the Bible are understood and evaluated primarily as historical evidence. The Bible is treated as an object of evidence, regardless of one's place in the theological spectrum of views about its authority. Some conservative

Christian scholars defend the Bible as historical evidence that proves their views. Other more liberal Christian scholars point to the limitations and diversity of the historical evidence in the Bible in support of their views. In either case, it is *the Bible as historical evidence* that matters. When it is read in this way, the Bible points away from itself and toward the history which created the evidence. The significance of the Bible is not understood to lie in the shape of the contents of the Bible itself but in the reconstructed history behind the text.

In the second chapter we examined the limitations of two common ways in which committed Christians have seen the Bible as evidence: the Bible as facts of revelation and the Bible as events of revelation. We discovered that these views have difficulty in reflecting the rich array of ways in which God has spoken and continues to speak through the Bible to the people of God in communities of faith.

For example, chapter two mentioned the category mistake of treating the Psalms as historical writing rather than as poetry. While we can examine the poetry of the Psalms as historical evidence of the religion of Israel when it was composed, such study is not likely to provide us with an understanding of its later use by Christians as "the prayer book" of the Bible,[15] nor of its theological and spiritual significance. Rather, it is precisely the issue that the Psalms were written as poetry, instead of as historical narratives, that makes it difficult to use them to reconstruct the history behind the text.

Almost every psalm has been the focus of unresolved historical debate, as to whether it was written before or after Israel's deportation into Babylon. (The most notable exception to this is Psalm 137, which begins "By the rivers of Babylon—there we sat down and there we wept when we remembered Zion"!) The poetic form of the Psalms, which limits their usefulness as a source for historical reconstruction of Israel's past, is precisely the same form that enhances their usefulness as spiritual guides to the people of God to whom they have spoken for thousands of years. Therefore, to think of the Bible primarily in the category of historical evidence is to miss much of the significance it possesses as Scripture for the people of God.

We will label this overidentification of the Bible and history as historicism. Of course, it is true that the Bible was formed in history and is used as Scripture by communities of Jews and Christians in history. The issue, however, is that large parts of the Bible itself have not been read and are not being read as history by those who use them in communities of faith. Thus to read the Bible primarily as historical evidence—with a focus on the world behind the text—provides only a part of the picture of its use as Scripture.

Historicism poses a serious danger for biblical interpretation and the development of Christian doctrine. The spiritual power of the Bible as Scripture is lost to the church amid sterile "scientific" debates which only consider how the Bible is to be understood in relation to its historical past. The capacity of God's Word to speak to the people of God is easily ignored in an environment dominated by an exclusive concern for the Bible as historical evidence.

Is there a way we can reject the danger of historicism without losing the connections between Christian faith and history? How can we keep the insights that historical-critical approaches provide about the formation of the Bible without losing the spiritual vitality and power of Scripture in the life of communities of faith? Canonical hermeneutics offers a postcritical perspective that can help us with these challenging questions.

Recovering the archaeology of the text. As the living Word of God, the Bible has a long history and a future direction. In order to understand how God is continuing to speak through Scripture to the people of God today, we need to dig deeply into the past. We should always remember that we are not the first people to whom God has spoken through these specific writings which now make up the canon of Scripture! In our discussion of canon as the rule of Scripture earlier in this chapter, we observed that the church's use of canon may be divided into two periods: (1) the long process of the formation of the canon into its final forms and (2) the period, up to and including the present, in which the canon of Scripture has continued to be recognized and read as the vehicle through which God speaks to the people of God.

As we explore the excavations of historical-critical interpretation of the Bible, it might be helpful to think of our study of the first period (the process of canon formation) as an examination of "the archaeology of the text." This phrase, borrowed from the French philosopher Paul Ricoeur,[16] provides us with a vivid image of the process of digging into the traces of the past. If we wish to discover how these specific books which we recognize as canon were shaped into their present forms, we need to excavate to find the fragmentary world behind the text. In this process there is no substitute for the painstaking labors of historical-critical study. Although these historical reconstructions of the past are always subject to change and should never be regarded as final, they represent our only means of access to the "earthen vessels"[17] in which the canon was formed.

Beyond its value in assisting us to trace the development of biblical texts to their final forms, historical-critical interpretation also serves an important practical function. It helps to restrain us from making the Bible mean whatever we would like to read into it from our personal and cultural situation. Historical-critical interpretation reminds us of the historical distance between ourselves and the Bible. The struggling, culturally marginal Hellenistic churches of the New Testament were not "just like" our tax-exempt, culturally accepted American denominational churches today. While the Bible certainly addresses our situation and contemporary world, we must be careful of the danger of reading our cultural assumptions directly into the text without being aware of the distance of time and space through which our interpretation of Scripture must travel. Many different "horizons of meaning"[18] separate our world—our contemporary horizon of meaning—from the worlds of the writers and editors of the various books of the Bible.

Thus canonical hermeneutics includes the changing insights of historical-critical study of the Bible as *part* of its larger, postcritical perspective. Just as there is more to our physical world than simply what is buried under the land and sea, so there is more to the world of the text than simply its "archaeology." Beyond the limitations of the world behind the text, with its historically reconstructed original traditions and events, lie the broader worlds of the communities of faith which have recognized and used the final forms of the biblical texts as Scripture for centuries. Canonical hermeneutics includes all of these worlds with their additional horizons of meaning, along with the world behind the text, in a multidimensional model of biblical interpretation.

Such a comprehensive perspective raises an important issue. How does one maintain control with all of these many different possibilities for meaning? What is to prevent the traditional interpretation of any particular historical horizon of meaning (e.g., the ancient horizon of the Roman emperor Constantine's era, the early medieval horizon of the Holy Roman Emperor Charlemagne's era, the Reformation horizon of John Calvin's Geneva or Elizabeth I's England) from arbitrarily dominating the process, especially if some of its views happen to fit in well with the background or wishes of the person doing the interpretation today?

Canonical hermeneutics responds to this concern by asserting that all biblical interpretation should begin and end with the test of making sense of the final forms of the text in light of the whole canon of Scripture. While there is an important place for historically reconstructed forms of the texts and selected historical emphases within this multidimensional model of interpretation, the canon of Scripture as used by communities of faith should provide the beginning and ending boundaries for interpretation.

In summary, on the one hand, the insights of historical-critical interpretation into the process of the formation of the canon ("the archaeology of the text"), with their practical function of restraining our understanding of the Bible from meaning whatever we and our culture would like, play an essential role in a canonical interpretation of the Bible. On the other hand, because of the danger of historicism (which overidentifies the Bible and history), historical-critical interpretation occupies a limited space in a canonical model. Historical criticism is not the goal of exegesis in a canonical context, but rather an important stage in a larger process. Canonical hermeneutics thus creates some room for a postcritical relationship between historical-critical and traditional approaches to interpreting the Bible. Through a reframing of tradition and a rehabilitation of typology, traditional exegesis of biblical texts finds a place alongside historical-critical exegesis in the interpretation of the Bible as Scripture. Both the buried treasures of traditional interpretation and the excavations of historical-critical interpretation are included in a balanced canonical model.

The Flowering Gardens: Postcritical Interpretation

Our explorations of the surroundings of the country, following the road markers of Scripture and canon, have led us from the buried treasures of traditional interpretation through the excavations of historical-critical investigation. Before we finish our survey we must take a brief tour through a few of the flowering gardens of postcritical interpretation.

Unlike the other approaches to interpretation, which have been shaped and refined over centuries, postcritical interpretation is a recent development. These gardens have been planted for only a short time and are not yet covered with the dust of history. It is too early to tell which of the many flowering plants are annuals, here this season and gone the next, and which will be perennials, back year after year. Furthermore, amid all the blooming plants, it is a difficult challenge to attempt to sort out the flowers from the weeds.

Despite these limitations, we will organize our tour around two major areas in which the postcritical perspective of canonical hermeneutics can strengthen our understanding of Scripture. First, we will examine some ways in which Christians discern the purposes of Scripture. We will see how the focus of canonical hermeneutics on the use of Scripture offers us a valuable approach for describing its authority. Then we will turn to the question of patterns of Scripture. Instead of resting biblical interpretation upon chains of prooftexts, canonical hermeneutics enables us to discover patterns within the canon which guide our journey toward a biblically based understanding of Christian doctrine.

Purposes of Scripture. Christians believe that God has given the Bible as a unique book to fulfill a variety of purposes. As 2 Timothy 3:16-17 declares, "All Scripture is inspired by God and is useful for teaching, for reproof, for correction, and for training in righteousness, so that everyone who belongs to God may be proficient, equipped for every good work." We maintain that not only does God speak to us through Scripture for the purpose of bringing us to salvation in Jesus Christ (2 Tim 3:15), but God continues to speak to us through Scripture throughout our Christian lives.

When we ask the question *why* God speaks in these particular books with an authority not found in others, our responses become more diverse. Although we may agree that God also speaks to us through literature such as sermons, devotional readings, Bible study materials, spiritual classics, poetry and novels, there is a special authority which we ascribe to God's speaking to us through Scripture. On what do we base our claim for this special authority of the Bible—an authority which goes beyond that of any other literature which we may encounter in our life together as Christians? How do we know that God has spoken and continues to speak to us in a uniquely authoritative way through the Bible?

Evangelical Christians have typically given three kinds of answers to these questions. The first answer makes a rhetorical appeal to the Bible itself: "The Bible says it. I believe it. That settles it." The reference to the Bible in this response begs the question. One could certainly identify many religious works besides the Bible (e.g., the Qur'an, Joseph Smith's *The Book of Mormon*,[19] Mary Baker Eddy's *Science and Health with a Key to the Scriptures*[20]) that claim God's special authority. Christians who give this sort of answer really are not referring so much to the Bible as they are referring to their own experience of the authority of the Bible. What their response commonly means is that they know through their own personal experience or through the authority of a few particular leaders in their church that God speaks to them through the Bible, and that settles the matter. They do not need to talk or think about it any further. Such an answer is really a form of blind faith or fideism.

The second kind of answer also appeals to the Bible but in a more nuanced way: "I know from the facts or events of the Bible that God has spoken to us through the Bible." In the second chapter we examined some of the problems of interpreting the Bible primarily as a collection of facts of revelation or events of revelation. Since the facts or events contained in a book are dependent on the contexts to which it refers, as well as the contexts of its author(s), transmitter(s) and readers, one is soon confronted with the necessity of specifying "whose version" of the facts or events is being considered. To take a simple example, whose version of the biblical accounts of the death of Judas should be believed—that found in Matthew 27:5 or that found in Acts 1:18 or some combination?

Once this context dependence is seen, then the appeal to the "historical evidence" becomes transformed into an appeal to *one's interpretation* of the evidence (or that of some other witnesses or experts upon whom one relies). The reliance on the facts or events of revelation commonly becomes reduced to an appeal to the interpreter's subjective judgment or simply to blind faith (fideism). The issue of personal *experience* seems to be inevitably present.

The third answer typically given by evangelical Christians to the question of the unique authority of the Bible is a direct appeal to personal religious experience: "I know that the Bible is *true for me* (or for my church). That is everything that I need to know (or everything that I can know)." This kind of response leads to a relativism that undermines the unique authority of the Bible. What is true in the experience of one person may not be true in the experience of another. As a result, the Bible becomes authoritative for some people, but not for others.

If we compare these three answers to the issue of the Bible's unique authority, we notice a striking similarity. Although only the third response appeals solely to the personal religious experience of the responder, it soon becomes apparent that all three kinds of answers are dependent on this experience. Even though some evangelical Christians might claim that they are just believing the "objective" facts or events of the Bible, such claims include a hidden reliance on personal experience.

If our understanding of the special authority which underlies the purposes of Scripture is to be based on more than the particular religious experiences of individuals and their religious communities, then a new kind of response is needed. Canonical hermeneutics offers a different perspective on the issue. The unique authority of the Bible is based on its *use* as Scripture by diverse communities of faith, both in the past and in the present.

The use of the Bible as Scripture by communities of faith is a practice which is clearly observable from both inside the community of believers and outside the community. One who is not a member of a community of faith which accepts the authority of the Bible still can acknowledge that communities of Jews and Christians use the Bible as Scripture.

Furthermore, grounding the Bible's authority upon its use as Scripture does not require that Christians either have an attitude of blind faith (fideism) or maintain an attitude of relativism toward those outside the community. As canonical Scripture, the Bible speaks both in support of and against the personal experience of the members of the community (including its human leaders). Thus the presence of both judgment and grace (God's no and God's yes[21]) in the life of a community ruled by the Bible as Scripture challenges approaches based on blind faith. In addition, an acceptance of the universal scope of the witness of the canon as a whole contends against any efforts to reduce the claims of Christianity to mere relativism. For example, communities which hear and respond to the universality of Isaiah 49:6 and Matthew 28:19-20 are unlikely to succumb to a complacent relativism regarding their role in God's mission of salvation.

A canonical perspective may be articulated from either side of the church's theological point of view. Looking from the human side *(coram humanibus),* the Bible's authority is dependent on the ways it has functioned and still functions as Scripture in the life of the Christian community. Describing matters from the divine side *(coram Deo),* the authority of Scripture expresses the purposes for which God gave the Scriptures to the people of God.

In summary, we have examined some of the limitations of typical evangelical responses to the issue of the unique authority of Scripture raised by its variety of purposes. Canonical hermeneutics with its focus on the use of the Bible as Scripture, observable from both within and outside the community, offers a valuable way of describing the special authority which God has given and Christian communities have recognized in these particular books of holy Scripture.

Patterns of Scripture. Since evangelical Christians place such a strong emphasis on the primary authority of Scripture for Christian life and thought, evangelical approaches to Christian doctrine not surprisingly include a strenuous effort to base all Christian teachings on specific references to the Bible. This commonly leads to the practice of prooftexting, which attempts to support any particular doctrinal assertion with a mass of related biblical references.

Such prooftexting is especially evident in many of the Reformation and post-Reformation confessions of the sixteenth and seventeenth centuries (e.g., the Lutheran Confession of Augsburg, the Reformed Westminster Confession). A particularly dramatic twentieth-century example of this approach is the "Baptist Faith and Message" statement of 1925 (revised 1963). Each article describes a given doctrine or practice, followed by a lengthy list of prooftexts.

Although prooftexting has been a common method of biblical interpretation since the time of the early church,[22] its use in support of Christian doctrine has always revealed limitations. Perhaps the greatest difficulty is posed by the problem that in a contest between two conflicting doctrinal interpretations simply compiling the greatest number of prooftexts does not necessarily mean that one has the correct biblical view.

A dramatic illustration of this difficulty may be found in the great fourth-century controversy over the doctrine of God led by Arius and Athanasius of Alexandria.[23] Arius argued that the Son of God, instead of being eternal God by nature, was created by God the Father from nothing. In contrast, Athanasius held that the Son was coeternal and "of one substance" with the Father. In other words, Athanasius supported the full divinity of Jesus Christ.

In the end, Athanasius's view of God as expressed in the doctrine of the Trinity won the day. The church judged this view to be a more faithful expression and elaboration of the Bible's teaching about God. The irony, however, is that the Arian side clearly had more and better biblical prooftexts. One could hardly imagine clearer biblical support for Arius's view than Colossians 1:15. In his hymn to Christ, Paul declares, "He is the image of the invisible God, *the firstborn of all creation.*"

Why then does Athanasius's view come to represent biblical orthodoxy? Athanasius's trinitarian doctrine of God represents the biblical insight that "only God can save." Christ must be fully God if he is going to be able to save humanity from sin. This biblical message is what the orthodox doctrine of the Trinity seeks to protect. Athanasius's view of God is more biblical, not because it has more prooftexts, but because it fits the *pattern* of the God who saves us in Jesus Christ, which is made known in Scripture.

Therefore, it is the patterns of Scripture which offer the key to a deeper understanding of biblical authority than that which can be obtained through prooftexting Christian doctrines. The discovery of patterns—the ways in which different parts come together to make a whole—is a basic element in the process by which we as humans perceive and claim to know meaning in the world.[24] Canonical hermeneutics maintains that the process of recognizing and describing the patterns we find in the Bible is at the heart of understanding the Bible's authority in a deeper way than that afforded by the historical reconstruction of critical scholarship.[25]

Thus, canonical hermeneutics is postcritical. It does not deny the insights of critical scholarship but seeks to incorporate them into a larger pattern. This emphasis on pattern in canonical hermeneutics also finds affinity with traditional interpretation of the Bible, especially with the use of typology to highlight similar situations between diverse biblical texts. Canonical hermeneutics incorporates both traditional and critical biblical interpretation into its more comprehensive perspective.

For example, in the third chapter we examined how Brevard Childs's canonical interpretations of the books of Amos and Ephesians included critical discussions about the authorship of these books but went beyond such authorship issues. The canonical Amos and the canonical Paul are larger than the Amos and Paul reconstructed by historical scholarship. When the figures of Amos and Paul are interpreted canonically, much of the richness of traditional biblical interpretation is able to be included in the portraits that emerge from the final forms of these biblical books. The canonical Amos proclaims God's judgment and mercy, not just gloom and doom; and the canonical Paul's theology of the church is shaped by the book of Ephesians. Yet the historical distance established by the incorporation of critical scholarship poses a check on the flights of fancy that emerge in traditional interpretation. We see the humanity and cultural shaping of these two historical figures through whose lives God speaks to us.

Our brief tour of the flowering gardens of postcritical interpretation has sought to show how canonical hermeneutics enables us to deepen our understanding of the purposes and patterns of Scripture. A more comprehensive picture of biblical authority, focusing on the use of the Bible as Scripture, seeks to embrace and then go beyond our narrow preoccupations with inspiration and prooftexting. As we have explored the surroundings of the country of interpretation, we have discovered a larger theological vision that encompasses all of the territory we surveyed: the buried treasures of traditional interpretation, the excavations of historical-critical investigations and the flowering gardens of postcritical scholarship.

Now that we have developed a more encompassing notion of biblical authority and a sharper insight into the patterns of truth contained within the canon, we are ready to proceed to the final stage of our journey from the Bible to doctrine. We are ready to see if we can catch a better glimpse of the great destination of our pilgrimage: the mystery of God.

5. Glimpsing the Destination
The Doctrine of God

THE GOAL OF OUR JOURNEY IS now on the horizon. As we draw nearer to it, we become aware that the mystery of God is greater than we can ever comprehend. We cannot grasp God with our limited minds; we can only glimpse God through the eyes of a faith which seeks understanding. The greatness of God always reaches beyond our human ways of knowing. "For as the heavens are higher than the earth, so are my ways higher than your ways and my thoughts than your thoughts" (Is 55:9).

Christians who attempt to speak of the doctrine of God should approach this awesome task with humility. There is no place for arrogant self-assertion or self-righteous certainty in the quest to deepen our knowledge of the mystery of God. Theologies which appear to have God all wrapped up in a neat conceptual package betray themselves. The "God" in their box is a lifeless idol, not the dynamic, living God revealed in the Scriptures. The Bible points toward the Lord who breaks through all of the categories within which people have tried to contain God.

Christian theology does not approach the doctrine of God in a vacuum. A long history of God's presence in Jesus Christ through the power of the Holy Spirit shapes the ways in which Christian communities have begun to know God. Since our faith precedes and undergirds our understanding, we do not approach God as an unknown stranger but as the triune God who already has graciously come to us. The God who created and redeemed us through Jesus Christ is the God we seek to know in Christian doctrine.

Thus our efforts to reflect on the doctrine of God in this chapter will focus on the doctrine of the Trinity. We will not be seeking to reflect on the one God as an abstract concept, but rather on God the three-in-one, whom Christians know through faith in Jesus Christ.[1]

Before we can explore the mystery of the Trinity directly, we need to examine the ways in which some questions of theological method shape our perspectives on the Trinity. We will be thinking about making the transition from "the country of interpretation" which we explored in the last chapter to our destination of doctrinal exposition in this chapter. We will look at the issues of preparation for the doctrine in Scripture, problems we encounter with the ancient language of the Trinity, and the purpose of Christian doctrine.

Then we will turn to a description of the doctrine of the Trinity. We will develop the theme that the Trinity is a "bounded mystery." Christian doctrine gives us boundaries within which we can explore the mystery of the Trinity. The truth of the doctrine of the Trinity can be discovered only within the paradoxes (seemingly contradictory ideas that taken together point to the truth) which it contains. We will consider three of these biblically shaped paradoxes: plurality (God is three and one), presence (God is already here and not yet present) and power (God is almighty and good).

Beyond thinking about the doctrine of the Trinity and its paradoxes, Christians celebrate the Trinity in song. The idea of canon is "transposed" from holy Scripture to heavenly praise. We will conclude our journey with a brief reflection on singing the doctrine of the Trinity.

Method: Perspectives on the Trinity

In the last chapter we explored the surroundings of the country of the theological interpretation of Scripture using the vehicle of canonical hermeneutics. Now we are faced with the task of making a transition to doctrinal exposition—the formal explanation of Christian doctrine. I have chosen to focus on the doctrine of the Trinity as our concrete example. Not only is this doctrine at the heart of our destination—a deeper glimpse of the mystery of God—but the notorious complexity of the Trinity makes it an ideal test case. For if we can make the transition from the Bible to doctrine with this difficult teaching about the mystery of God, the way should be clear for the development of a canonical approach to other areas of Christian doctrine.

Preparation in Scripture. A canonical approach to the doctrine of the Trinity would, of course, seek to begin with a careful examination of passages in the Bible that offer support for or challenge to the doctrine. In addition to the central New Testament passages, Old Testament views of God would need to be included. The long history of interpretation of these passages would also need to be examined, particularly the theological controversies of the fourth century, which led to the formal development of the doctrine.[2]

Since such a detailed study is beyond the scope of this book, we will simply focus on the major problem immediately raised by passages in the New Testament. The New Testament does not provide us with a fully developed description of the doctrine of God as Trinity. Instead, what we find are passages which describe God as threefold or triadic (e.g., Mt 28:19-20; Lk 3:22; 10:21-22; Jn 3:34-35; Rom 5:5-6; 2 Cor 13:13 [and parallel benedictions]; Jude 20-21). Other passages describe God in twofold or dyadic terms (e.g., Jn 1:1; 1 Cor 6:19; 8:6; 2 Cor 3:16-17).

Since the New Testament does not spell out all the details of the relationships between the Father, Son and Holy Spirit, we are left with the question of precisely how the Bible's teachings about God are connected with the more formal and technical statements of the doctrine of the Trinity. To take the famous fourth-century example of the Arian controversy, how do the many biblical passages about the relationship between God the Father and the Son (Jesus) connect with the trinitarian teaching that the Father and the Son are of the same essence *(homoousios)*—of "the same stuff"? Since the New Testament teaches that Jesus is "one" with the Father (e.g., Jn 10:30), how does this biblical truth fit together with the doctrinal teaching that the full divinity of Jesus Christ requires that as the Son of God he must be coeternal with God the Father?

One way to respond to these questions is to describe the biblical teachings about God as laying the foundations or preparing the way for the later development of the doctrine of the Trinity. In other words, the truth of the Bible is later more precisely specified, systematized and elaborated in the doctrinal formulations of the Trinity. If we want to maintain this understanding of *trinitarian preparation* in Scripture, we must be careful to distinguish our understanding of such biblical preparation from two related but inadequate views.

The first view makes too little of trinitarian preparation. It simply holds that the language of the doctrine of the Trinity is *permitted* by the language of Scripture. Of course, the history of the doctrine of the Trinity clearly shows that trinitarian language developed in the context of complicated debates over what the proper biblical understanding of God involved. Thus it is historically correct to say that the language of the Bible was interpreted to permit the development of the language of the doctrine of the Trinity. The problem is that, if we just follow this view, we could also argue (with lots of prooftexts—e.g., Prov 8:22; Col 1:15) that the language of the Bible was also interpreted to permit the development of the language of the heresy of Arianism. Therefore, taken by itself, the view that trinitarian language is permitted by the language of Scripture does not tell us enough about the direction of the development of the language of Scripture into Christian doctrine. Trinitarian preparation becomes reduced to simply one of many possibilities which the language of Scripture may be interpreted to support.

The second inadequate view makes too much of trinitarian preparation in Scripture. It claims that trinitarian language is *required* to understand properly the language of Scripture. The problem with this view is that it "discovers" trinitarian language implied in an amazing diversity of biblical passages in the New Testament and even in the Old Testament. In other words, later explicit trinitarian language is read back into the Bible. Perhaps the most famous example of this approach is Augustine's interpretation of the use of the first-person plural ("us" and "our") in Genesis 1:26 ("Let us make humankind in our image") as referring to the presence of the Trinity at the creation.[3] So instead of serving as a basis for later doctrinal development, the Bible is used as a collection of prooftexts to establish previously held doctrinal views.

A better understanding of trinitarian preparation in Scripture seeks a balance between the extremes offered by these two inadequate views. The language of the doctrine of the Trinity is understood to be *warranted* by the authoritative language of Scripture.[4] In other words, biblical teaching about God provides the reasons or grounds for the later development of trinitarian language. The canonical shape of biblical language justifies the later use of more technical trinitarian formulations.

A simple musical illustration might offer us a way to understand the diverse biblical language about God as preparation for the language of the Trinity. A musical triad consists of three notes, which when played together form one chord. For example, the notes "C," "E" and "G" when played together form a C major chord. The notes may be played one at a time in a sequence that fits together (e.g., "C" then "E" then "G"; or "G" then "E" then "C") or they may be played randomly. The notes may also be played dyadically, two at a time (e.g., "C" and "E" or "E" and "G" or "C" and "G").

When the writers of the New Testament described the God who had saved them in Jesus Christ, they characteristically used three different "notes"—God the Father, Jesus Christ the Son and the Holy Spirit. Frequently these notes were sounded one at a time. Sometimes two notes were sounded together as dyads. Occasionally, two notes were sounded, with the third coming in the next verse (e.g., Rom 5:5-6). The three notes could be sounded one at a time in a sequence (e.g., 1 Cor 12:4-6). Once in a while they were sounded all together as a triadic chord (e.g., Mt 28:19-20).

In summary, the language which the Bible uses to speak of God provides some preparation for the later development of the language of the doctrine of the Trinity. Trinitarian language is warranted by the language of Scripture. Now that we have considered some of the diversity of biblical language about God in relation to the Trinity, we next need to examine some of the difficulties with the classical doctrinal language itself.

Problems with language. How can we speak without contradiction of God as three (Father, Son, Spirit) and one at the same time? Christian theologians in the fourth century tried to respond to this challenge by shaping the New Testament triads into technical philosophical formulas. They moved from the threefold experience of God in salvation (known as the "economic" Trinity) to philosophical reflection on the being of God itself (known as the "immanent" or the "ontological" Trinity).

In the classic Greek formulation of the doctrine of the Trinity, God is three *hypostases* (distinct forms of appearing) in one *ousia* (essence). In the Latin "translation" (actually a different interpretation) of the Greek formula God is three *personae* (persons) in one *substantia* (substance). Both of these doctrinal definitions use the terminology of Plato's philosophy, as it was shaped by his successors in the ancient world (e.g., the philosophies of Middle Platonism and Neo-Platonism).

As we try to understand these doctrinal formulations today, this ancient philosophical language poses major difficulties because we see the world differently. If someone asks us what is "real"—the concrete individual (e.g., my dog Fido) or the universal category (e.g., the concept "dog")—we typically would choose the concrete individual (my dog Fido). We see universal categories as abstract concepts derived from concrete individuals. For most of us, the category "dog" is an abstraction derived from the characteristics of "real" individual dogs like my dog Fido.

Thinkers in the ancient world—including the theologians who formulated the doctrine of the Trinity—saw reality in the opposite way. Universals—like the perfect form of dog or the ideal of beauty— were what was real. Concrete individuals were imperfect embodiments of the real universals. So, to continue our examples, my dog Fido was an imperfect embodiment of the perfect form of dog; and the beautiful individual was an imperfect embodiment of the universal idea of beauty. Given this worldview, early Christian thinkers experienced particularly great difficulties with heresies that attempted to absorb the threeness of God into the oneness of God (e.g., the heresy of modalism, which will be discussed later in this chapter).

In contrast, most Christians who live in our individualistic Western world have difficulty understanding how God can be one if God is in three "persons." The threeness of God tends to divide the oneness of God (e.g., the heresy of tritheism or three gods, which we will also discuss later). Our modern tendency toward emphasizing God's threeness over God's oneness is strengthened by our view of what constitutes a person. A person is commonly seen as a distinct center of subjectivity (personal experience) with an individual personality. If we hear the doctrine of the Trinity's proclamation that God is three persons as meaning that God is three separate individuals, then it is nonsense to talk of one God. If we believe that the three members of the Trinity are three different personalities (three individual centers of subjectivity), then we have become polytheists who worship three gods.

Our tendency to emphasize God's threeness over God's oneness and to see persons as individual personalities has caused some major twentieth-century theologians to propose that Christians either replace the term *person* in the doctrine of the Trinity (e.g., Karl Barth, who favors "modes of existence"[5]) or explain it in a different way (e.g., Karl Rahner, who proposes to redefine persons as "distinct manners of subsisting"[6]).

The use of the term *person* clearly does need some reinterpretation if Christians are going to avoid becoming practical polytheists through their misunderstanding of the doctrine of the Trinity. Perhaps thinking of "persons" like characters in a Greek play might help a little. One actor, wearing different masks, appears as different characters (distinct forms of appearing). This does not solve the problem of keeping the unity of God's nature, but it does help to explain how one God can act in different forms (Father, Son, Spirit) in the world without being divided.

In any case, there are two important reasons for keeping the term *person* in the doctrine and explaining it, rather than replacing it. The first reason is the significant place that *person* holds in our traditions of music and worship. More evangelical Christians have probably learned about the doctrine of the Trinity from singing the hymn "Holy, Holy, Holy"[7] than from all of the books ever written about this doctrine, whether popular or technical. A more precise but also more abstract substitute for *person* (like Barth's "modes of existence") would not encourage Christians to seek to know more about this difficult doctrine. The awkwardness of singing "Holy, holy, holy; merciful and mighty; God in three [modes of existence], blessed Trinity!"[8] would only be magnified if one tried to use such terminology in any contemporary praise choruses which teach about the triune God.

The problem of substitution, however, goes deeper than these practical aesthetic dilemmas. For even if a musically smooth substitute could be found, the use of more abstract, impersonal terms would tend to increase the perceived distance between individuals and God. This distance is part of the cultural individualism and lack of community which fuel the problems we experience with the term *person*. We should avoid proposed solutions that will only worsen the problem!

The second reason for keeping the term *person* in the doctrine of the Trinity and explaining it is its inclusiveness. In a time when people are feeling excluded by the traditional language of Christian doctrine, especially its male imagery, the term *person* includes everyone—men and women, boys and girls. Even if we need to explain that, like other terms we use for God, *person* needs to be modified because of the differences between God and humanity, its familiar inclusiveness should be seen as an asset for Christian education.

Our discussion of some problems we experience today with the language of the doctrine of the Trinity leads us to consider a more general methodological issue: the purpose of the language of Christian doctrine.

Purpose of doctrine. Why do Christian communities need doctrines? Since the Scriptures are the final authority for our faith, why are doctrines necessary as well? During the early centuries of the Christian church, when the canon of the New Testament was still in the process of being formed, Christians realized the need for summaries of their faith. The processes of preaching and teaching the faith, of guarding churches from false teachings and of instructing new converts all contributed to the demand for the organization of the teachings of the faith into concise, consistent form. Particularly when baptisms occurred, a brief and authoritative summary of the Christian faith, which new Christians were professing, gradually developed as part of the baptismal service. Such summaries of the faith became known as "the rule of faith" (Latin *regula fidei*).

When the canonization process was drawing to a close and the books of the Christian Bible were approaching their final forms, Christians began to refer to the Scriptures as a whole as the rule of faith. This extended use of the term, however, did not end the need for summaries of the complex, lengthy and diverse teachings of the Bible. Confessions of faith, as well as binding creeds, continued to be identified by many Christians as part of the rule of faith. Continued reflection on and elaboration of the doctrines summarized in these creeds and confessions played a central role in the development of doctrinal theology in the church.

Christian theologies today display at least three distinct approaches to Christian doctrine.[9] Each of these approaches reflects a different understanding of the nature and function of doctrine—of what doctrine is and what doctrine does. The model of doctrine which underlies each approach shapes the type of theology that results.

The first model sees doctrine as providing objective information. Doctrines are propositions which state the facts of the Christian faith. The truth claims of the faith primarily concern realities which lie in the external world. This model of doctrine is equally applicable to theologies which seek to verify the facts of the Bible in the external world (e.g., the world was created in six days) and those which seek to make claims which go beyond the explicit story given in the Bible (e.g., the Virgin Mary was herself immaculately conceived).

As we discussed in the second chapter, there is great ambiguity in determining whose version of "the facts" is the correct one. Even more important, however, is to notice the change of focus away from the Bible and the teachings of the faith to the external world behind the Bible and doctrine. Christian theology of this sort is always either looking for evidence to confirm its claims or rather proudly claiming that the authority of its claims means that all evidence must be made to fit.

In contrast, the second model sees doctrine as the expression of subjective feelings. Doctrines are symbols of our inner Christian experience. What matters is the inner world of spiritual experience. Doctrine provides a way for the internal realities of faith to be symbolized publicly.

This model reduces Christian doctrine to Christian experience, whether individual or communal. The truth of doctrine becomes the truth of life experience. Connections with the Bible and with the historical traditions of Christianity offer illustrations of experience, rather than norms for belief. For instance, according to this model, the truth of the doctrine of the resurrection of Jesus Christ lies in its symbolizing our inner experience (i.e., Jesus lives within our hearts) rather than in its historical occurrence.

The third model sees doctrine as describing rules which are authoritative for Christian communities. Doctrines do not explain the mysteries of the faith; they regulate the language of the faith. Doctrines provide boundaries within which our reflection on the mysteries of our faith may occur.

Following this third model, monotheism (one God) is a rule that governs Christian talk about God.[10] In whatever way Christians talk about the mystery of God's threeness and God's oneness, they should be guided by the rule of monotheism; otherwise, they will become polytheists. The rule of monotheism does not reveal to us the metaphysical nature of God's oneness; nor does it tell us how we should relate God's oneness and God's threeness. Monotheism simply provides a boundary or a "negative guideline" that governs Christian language about God.

One way of understanding how this regulative view of Christian doctrine works is to think of doctrine as something like the "grammar of faith."[11] Grammar offers rules which govern the way we speak a language. If we violate the rules of grammar, we end up speaking ungrammatically and perhaps even incoherently. Grammar is not the object of language; rather grammar regulates how a community uses its language. The goal of learning the rules of grammar is that we may learn to speak properly, not that we will all become grammarians. We may speak grammatically without being able to reproduce consciously or recite in detail all the rules; they may have become internalized.

Similarly, doctrine may be understood as offering rules which govern the way we speak the language of faith. If we violate the rules of doctrine, we end up speaking heretically and perhaps even incoherently about the mystery of God. Doctrine is not the object of our faith; rather doctrine regulates how Christian communities use their language. The goal of learning the rules of doctrine is that we may learn to speak properly about the mystery of God, not that we will all become doctrinal theologians. We may speak in an orthodox way about the mystery of God without being able to reproduce consciously or recite in detail all of the rules of doctrine; they may become internalized.

Our canonical approach to theology places one important qualification on this regulative view of Christian doctrine. While a regulative view seems quite useful as a way to understand what doctrine is and does, it is not very helpful as a model for understanding the nature and function of Scripture. There are two reasons for this restriction.

The first reason is the nature of the Scriptures. The Scriptures are the rule of faith which forms and tests all the other rules of faith. As canon the Bible is the rule-making rule, the norm which shapes all the other norms.[12] In evangelical Christian communities, the Bible's status as Holy Scripture means that it is read and interpreted authoritatively in a different way from Christian doctrine. The Reformation watchword of "Scripture alone" *(sola Scriptura)* points to this special role of the Bible in Christian communities.

The second reason points to a more general weakness of this regulative view of doctrine. Understanding the Bible from this perspective can easily lead to a reading of the Bible that is cut off from the external historical world (the world behind the text) in which it was formed. Although, as we have seen, there is much more to a canonical reading of the Bible than the recovering of the archaeology of the text, the relationship between the Bible and the world behind the text is essential for the continuity of its role as the Word of God.

Our exploration of some issues of theological method which shape our understanding of the doctrine of the Trinity has focused on preparation for the doctrine in Scripture, our problems in understanding the ancient language and worldview of the Trinity, and the purpose of Christian doctrine. We are now ready to wrestle with some of the paradoxes that establish the boundaries of this great mystery of our faith.

Mystery: Paradoxes of the Trinity

At the heart of the great doctrines of Christianity lies the mystery of God. Teachings like the Incarnation—God's becoming a human person in Jesus Christ—and the Trinity function more like boundaries around a reality that is too great for human understanding than as complete explanations of the nature and work of God. We use the term *mystery* to describe a truth or reality so deep that our minds cannot fathom it, or so vast that we cannot comprehend it.

The mystery of God will be completely revealed only at the end time. We will see God clearly only when we are with God in eternity. In this earthly life the mystery of God can be known only in partial and fragmentary ways. Paul describes our situation in his great chapter on the love of God: "For now we see in a mirror, dimly, but then we will see face to face. Now I know only in part; then I will know fully, even as I have been fully known" (1 Cor 13:12).

Since Christian doctrine offers us rules or negative guidelines which set boundaries around the mystery of God, we need to look at history to see how these rules emerged. What is the historical process of the development of the Christian doctrine of the Trinity, and how does it connect with our understanding of the mystery of God today?

When we examine both ancient and contemporary understandings of the Trinity, we discover that they operate by means of paradox. The term *paradox* literally describes a belief which goes against received opinion (Greek: *para,* "against" and *doxa,* "opinion").[13] We are using paradox to describe statements that appear to be self-contradictory to common sense but yet are true. For example, when the doctrine of the Trinity proclaims that God is three persons yet one God, this is a paradoxical belief. The claim that God can be three and yet one at the same time appears self-contradictory to common sense, yet Christians believe that it is true.

Looking at the operation of this kind of paradox more closely, we notice that it sets up a field of tension between two extremes. For example, the threeness of God is in tension with the oneness of God. The paradoxical truth that the doctrine of the Trinity claims to describe lies *within* the field of tension created by the extremes. Taken by itself, each extreme leads to a false belief which contradicts the paradoxical truth of the Trinity. Thus the extremes provide negative guidelines, which set the boundaries within which the mystery of God can be explored. Of course, we must always remember that the mystery of God is greater than any of the paradoxes we use to describe it. Now we "know only in part." Our paradoxical knowing of the eternal God is inevitably finite and fragmentary.

We will be exploring three paradoxes of the Trinity. The paradox of plurality discovers truth in the tension between God as three and God as one. The paradox of presence points to the reality of God in the tension between God as "already" with us and "not yet" completely here. The paradox of power struggles with suffering in the tension between God as almighty and God as good.

Plurality: three and one. The tension between the claims that God is three (Father, Son and Holy Spirit) and that God is one (monotheism) creates the birthplace for the concept of the Trinity. As we discussed earlier in this chapter, although the Bible does not use the word *Trinity,* the Bible's description of God prepares the way for the later development of the doctrine. Specifically, the dyads and triads of the New Testament, when combined with a monotheism that does not see God as a monolith, provide scriptural warrant for the use of trinitarian language about God by early Christians.

The Greek apologist (defender of the faith) Theophilus of Antioch first used the Greek term *trias* or "Triad" to describe God around A.D. 180.[14] The word *trinity* (Latin *trinitas*) is a compound, formed by combining "tri-" (Latin *trini*) and "unity" (Latin *unitas*). The North African lawyer Tertullian of Carthage first used the word at the beginning of the third century, when he was arguing against a Monarchian heretic named Praxeas.[15] The Monarchians were Christians who, in their concern to protect the sovereignty ("monarchy") of God, overemphasized God's oneness and downplayed God's threeness.

As the orthodox leaders of the early church formally developed the doctrine of the Trinity in the fourth century, they became aware of two opposing dangers which threatened their balanced formulation of the doctrine.[16] Like the Monarchians, one could overemphasize the oneness of God at the expense of the threeness of God. The group which posed this danger most gravely was the modalistic Monarchians, or modalists for short. (This group was also sometimes known as the Sabellians, after the name of one of their leaders, Sabellius.) The modalists believed that the Trinity was composed of three modes of being, each of which was simply an appearance or manifestation of the one God. This view threatened to reduce the threeness of God to little more than one God who appeared at different times in various forms on the earth.

The opposite danger to modalism is that one could emphasize the threeness of God at the expense of the oneness of God—the danger of tritheism. Tritheism simply means that Christians worship three individual gods (the Father, Son and Holy Spirit) who are related to another but not of the same stuff (or of the same essence—*homoousios*—as the Nicene Fathers described it). In today's highly individualistic society, many Christians are tritheists, who think that the Trinity consists of three independent members. The Father, Son and Holy Spirit become three individual centers of subjectivity.

Athanasius and the other leaders of the orthodox party in the fourth century were involved in fighting Arianism (which subordinated the Son to the Father), rather than tritheism. Yet we can see that for some of these formulators of the doctrine like Gregory of Nyssa,[17] tritheism was an important boundary marker for the doctrine of the Trinity. If the Trinity was reduced to three independent gods, then Christianity was in danger of becoming polytheism, as its Jewish (and later Muslim) critics were quick to point out.

Modalism (emphasizing God's oneness over God's threeness) and tritheism (emphasizing God's threeness over God's oneness) not only are opposing dangers to the doctrine of the Trinity, but they serve as negative guidelines for the truth of doctrine. The tension between the oneness and threeness of God—in which the paradoxical truth of the Trinity lies—is bounded by the extremes of these heresies. If theological exploration of the doctrine of the Trinity is to remain orthodox, it must observe these boundary markers. Christian theology, whether ancient or modern, can relate the oneness and threeness of God in any of a variety of ways, within the limits represented by *both* of these negative guidelines.

Imagine, for instance, that you are piloting a large boat down a river. Colored buoys mark the dangerous shallows near each riverbank. You are free to navigate your boat anywhere within the deep channel of the river. In fact, it is likely that you will find yourself navigating closer to the buoys on one side or the other. Nevertheless, if you do not want to ground your boat on the perilous shallows, you must navigate in the channel between the boundary markers.

In similar fashion, Christian theological reflection on the mystery of God must steer carefully between the opposing perils of modalism and tritheism. It will probably drift toward one or the other, but it must navigate between them. The modern comparison of the Trinity to the self (the psychological analogy of the Trinity) by theologians like Karl Rahner[18] drifts toward modalism, while staying within the channel of orthodoxy. In contrast, the modern comparison of the Trinity to community (the social analogy of the Trinity) by theologians like Leonard Hodgson[19] and Jürgen Moltmann[20] drifts toward tritheism, while seeking to stay in the mainstream of theological reflection. If Christian theology is not to dissolve God's threeness into God's oneness or lose God's oneness in God's threeness, it must observe the negative guidelines on both sides.

Presence: already and not yet. A second biblically shaped paradox of the doctrine of the Trinity is the paradox of God's presence. As Christians we experience God as already present with us and yet still coming to be with us. The coming of Jesus Christ into the world vividly illustrates this paradoxical tension. On the one hand, through the Incarnation, as the Word made flesh, Christ has come to be with us. In his birth, life, death and resurrection Jesus has already been with us, and in the presence and power of the Holy Spirit Christ is present with us today. Yet, on the other hand, as Christians we live in the hope of Christ's second coming. Christ has not yet returned. At the end of the age he will come again in the fullness of his glory. So we live between the comings of Christ. Christ has already come; Christ is not yet fully come.

When we study Jesus' proclamation of the kingdom of God in the New Testament, especially in the Synoptic Gospels (Matthew, Mark and Luke), we find another clear example of this paradox of the presence of God. Is the kingdom of God a present reality or a future expectation for Jesus? The answer is that the kingdom of God is paradoxically both present and future. The kingdom is both already here and not yet fully come. This tension between "already" and "not yet" accounts for the way in which Jesus proclaims God's message to the people: "Repent, for the kingdom of heaven has come near," or alternatively, "the kingdom of heaven is at hand" (Mt 3:2 and parallels).

Understanding this biblical tension between the "already" and the "not yet" of God's presence provides a key for analyzing the strengths and weaknesses of some of the major approaches to the doctrine of God held by Christians today. The paradox of presence offers us negative guidelines for evaluating whether a particular theological view of God preserves a biblical balance or provides only a one-sided view of the mystery of God.

First, we will look at some theologies which overemphasize the "already" of God's presence at the expense of the "not yet." Since the High Middle Ages certain theologies have sought to express the doctrine of God in the form of logical propositions. Such theologies claim to deduce these logical propositions with certainty from God's revelation.

Roman Catholic theologies of this kind are often labeled scholastic theologies because of the medieval philosophical schools in which they were developed. The revelation of God is contained in logical propositions that have been derived from the teaching office of the church (called the magisterium), which holds the responsibility and power for interpreting the deposit of Scripture and tradition.

Protestant theologies of this kind are also often (and perhaps incorrectly) labeled Protestant scholasticism. Their understanding of God's revelation is expressed in logical propositions, which they claim to derive directly from the proper interpretation of the Bible. Creeds, confessions of faith and other church traditions are to be tested by their agreement with this proper interpretation of Scripture.

Theologies of propositional revelation—whether Protestant or Catholic—understand God as "already" defined. God's revelation in the past, as deduced and defined by logical propositions, determines the nature of God's presence now and in the future. The God of propositional revelation is not only unchangeable but capable of being perceived in a strictly rational manner, based on the "scientific" facts of revelation.

Therefore theologies that see God in terms of logical propositions alone have broken the biblical tension between the "already" and the "not yet." The paradox of the presence of God has been dissolved in favor of the "already." In such propositional theologies, the "not yet" of God's future coming has been subordinated or eliminated in favor of the God who has been "already" defined in the past.

In direct contrast to propositional theologies, we will now briefly examine an approach to theology which overemphasizes the "not yet" at the expense of the "already." This twentieth-century American theology is known as process theology. We will be particularly concerned with the early experience-based version of process theology developed by theologians like Schubert Ogden[21] and John Cobb.[22]

Following the insights of the process philosopher Alfred North Whitehead,[23] these theologians understand God, as well as nature and humanity, to be in the process of development. The being of God is not a static substance, but a dynamic event of "becoming." God is understood to be in all things (panentheism). The biblical tension between God and the world has been changed into a correlation, in which the processes of God and the world are interdependent. The "lure" of the future replaces clear beginnings and endings of history.

Process theology's emphasis on the "not yet" dissolves the "already" of God's presence. God the Father, the Son and the Spirit become a collection of rather loosely related and replaceable symbols for God, rather than forming the Trinity. If the God of propositional revelation is defined too restrictively by deductions from the past, the God of process theology is defined too openly by the future. In both cases, the paradoxical tension between the "already" and the "not yet" of God's presence has been broken. A biblically shaped understanding of the Trinity needs to affirm both the "already" and the "not yet" of God's paradoxical presence.

Christian theology in the twentieth century has witnessed a number of attempts to find some middle ground between the boundaries of the "already" and the "not yet." Roman Catholic theology saw the development of a modified propositional theology by theologians like Bernard Lonergan and Karl Rahner.[24] Twentieth-century Protestant theology challenged propositionalism with the events-of-revelation approach of the Biblical Theology movement,[25] which was discussed in chapter two, as well as with the "encounter" theology of Emil Brunner and other Protestant thinkers.[26]

The most dramatic attempt to rethink the paradox of God's presence has occurred in the development of eschatological (of last things) theology by German theologians like Jürgen Moltmann[27] and Eberhard Jüngel.[28] This approach attempts to preserve the biblical tension between the "already" and "not yet" of God's presence by focusing on the cross of Christ. Following Martin Luther's theology of the cross, the death of God is identified with the crucifixion of Christ. As Jesus cries out, "My God, my God, why have you forsaken me?" (Mt 27:46, quoting Ps 22:1), Christians experience both the presence and the absence of God.

This view of "the crucified God" (Moltmann) raises questions about the adequacy of such language to lead us to know God's presence. When does this language stop being paradoxical and become simply contradictory? What is to ensure that the language of eschatological theology does not become merely an elaborate linguistic illusion that projects our human needs on God?

The attempt of eschatological theology to grasp the paradox of God's presence reveals that a perfect balance between the "already" and the "not yet" seems beyond the limits of human language. Like all those who search to find a middle ground between the boundaries of a God who is already defined and a God who is not yet defined, theologians who seek to explore the paradox of God's presence are called to the humility of prayer and praise.

Power: almighty and good. A third biblically shaped paradox of the doctrine of the Trinity relates to the nature of God's power. The idea that God is almighty (omnipotent or all-powerful) is in tension with the idea that God is good. We see this tension most clearly in the questions raised by the experience of suffering.

When people suffer, they commonly ask questions like "Why is this happening to me?" or "Why is this happening now?"[29] These questions reveal a deep need to understand, explain or at least rationalize the experience. If the suffering is innocent—as in the story of Job or, more deeply, in the cross of Jesus—these "why" questions become all the more insistent. The questions may literally be screamed out of the midst of our pain and loss.

For persons who believe in God these questions ultimately focus on God's nature and actions. The classic expression of the dilemma is "How can a God who is both almighty and good allow such unjust suffering in the world?" If God is almighty, then God should have the power to stop or prevent such suffering; if God is good, then God must have the desire to eliminate this suffering. Therefore either God does not want to end suffering (in which case God seems evil, rather than good) or God cannot prevent or stop suffering (in which case God seems not to be all-powerful).

Christian philosophers and theologians label this dilemma the problem of "theodicy" (God's justice).[30] It is important to remember that such a problem makes sense only if we assume the existence of God. Otherwise, it is not surprising that the response to suffering in a godless universe should be "sound and fury, signifying nothing." The problem of God's justice is a problem for those of us who believe in God.

The history of Christian doctrine teaches us that to affirm only one side of the paradox of God as almighty and good leads into distortion of biblical views of God. On the one side, Christians who affirm the almighty power of God but who reject God's goodness are left with two unsatisfactory alternatives. The first is to claim a belief in one all-powerful God who wills evil. Such a malevolent divinity is a God who may command our fear, but not a God who is worthy of our loving worship. This is not the loving heavenly Father to whom Jesus prayed. The second alternative is to claim a belief in two Gods (dualism). One God is evil, and the other is good. Since the heresy of Marcion in the second century, which identified the evil God with the Old Testament Creator and the good God with the Father of Jesus the redeemer, Christians have rejected this view. Such a view sacrifices the oneness of God (monotheism) for an intellectual "solution" to the problem of God's relationship to suffering.

On the other side, a number of Jews and Christians today, like Rabbi Kushner[31] and Protestant process theologians,[32] urge that we should affirm the goodness of God and reject the almightiness of God. This view is commonly defended out of a compassion for the experience of those in the midst of innocent suffering. An all-powerful God seems distant and uncaring to persons experiencing the powerlessness of their suffering. Thus, according to this view, Christians should give up (or at least severely restrict) God's almightiness in favor of a good God who identifies with those trapped in suffering. Once again the paradoxical biblical view of God is rejected in favor of a simpler view that embraces one side of the dilemma.

A trinitarian perspective offers a more biblically balanced response to the questions of God's relationship to suffering. In the mystery of the relationship between the Father, the Son and the Spirit, we find expressed the dynamic, self-giving love which reveals God's nature and actions.[33] The relationship between the Father and the Son on the cross offers the key to God's costly identification with human suffering.[34]

One way of picturing this trinitarian approach to the problem of God's relationship to suffering is to imagine a cross in the heart of God. If we want to know God's true nature, we should not picture an aloof almightiness nor a powerless goodness, but a cross. The cross shows us that self-giving love, revealed in the tension between God's almightiness and God's goodness, is the central theme of God's relationship to suffering.

Of course, we are not saying that this trinitarian approach "solves" or explains the problem of God's justice for Christians. No, our questions about the incomprehensibility of innocent suffering remain. Like Job we discover that there are no satisfying answers to questions born out of the agony of innocent suffering (Job 38—41). "Where were you when I laid the foundation of the earth? Tell me, if you have understanding" (Job 38:4).

What has changed is that our questions have a home. They are now located within the paradox of God's almightiness and goodness. The Christian doctrine of the Trinity enables us to put some boundaries around the questions of suffering, which point us into the heart of the mystery of God.

Music: Praises to the Trinity
"Then I looked, and I heard the voice of many angels surrounding the throne and the living creatures and the elders; they numbered myriads of myriads and thousands of thousands, singing with full voice" (Rev 5:11-12).

Our journey from the Bible to Christian doctrine ends in musical praise. A canon of heavenly song arises from the canon of Holy Scripture. It is not accidental that the Scriptures picture heaven as filled with the sung praise of God. For there comes a time when the limited and ultimately inadequate ways in which we think and speak about God (Is 55:8-9) are surpassed by the praise of God.

The mystery of God is so great that finally we are confronted with our inability even to conceive of God, let alone adequately to explain the trinitarian mystery of our faith. When we face this human limitation, we have two choices. Either we approach our Lord in silent contemplation or we sing our grateful praise (Ps 100:4). Finally, the great mystery of God, the Trinity, calls for contemplation or celebration, rather than mere explanation.

The history of Christian doctrine has been characterized by the slogan "The law of praying is the law of believing" *(lex orandi, lex credendi).* In other words, the ways in which we worship God shape the ways in which we believe and think about God. The language of worship shows the way for the language of doctrine. For many evangelical Christians, this slogan should perhaps be modified to declare, "The law of singing is the law of believing" *(lex cantandi, lex credendi).*[35] For the heart of our faith is often most fully expressed in song. Like prayer, singing joins our hearts and minds together in the worship of God.

So as we complete our pilgrimage with these glimpses of the paradoxical mystery of the doctrine of the Trinity, it is right and fitting that we should praise the Triune God:

Holy, holy, holy! Lord God Almighty!
Early in the morning our song shall rise to Thee;
Holy, holy, holy; merciful and mighty!
God in three Persons, blessed Trinity![36]

Notes

An asterisk (*) placed before a title in the notes indicates that the work is included in the bibliography with further annotation.

Chapter 1: Beginning the Journey

[1]Saint Bonaventure, *The Mind's Road to God,* trans. George Boas (Indianapolis: Bobbs-Merrill, 1953). A more recent translation, entitled *The Soul's Journey into God,* may be found in the Paulist Classics of Western Spirituality series: Bonaventure, *The Soul's Journey into God, The Tree of Life, The Life of St. Francis,* trans. Ewert Cousins (New York: Paulist, 1978), pp. 51-116.

[2]See Hans-Georg Gadamer's analysis of "the classical" in *Truth and Method,* ed. Garrett Barden and John Cumming (New York: Seabury, 1975), pp. 253-58. David Tracy offers a clear, concise introduction to Gadamer's philosophical hermeneutics in "Interpretation of the Bible and Interpretation Theory," in Robert M. Grant with David Tracy, *A Short History of the Interpretation of the Bible,* rev. ed. (Philadelphia: Fortress, 1984), pp. 154-60.

[3]A more detailed discussion of the doctrine of the Trinity from the perspective of canonical hermeneutics is offered in chapter five.

[4]Josef Bleicher, *Contemporary Hermeneutics: Hermeneutics as Method, Philosophy and Critique* (Boston: Routledge and Kegan Paul, 1980), and Richard Palmer, *Hermeneutics: Interpretation Theory in Schleiermacher, Dilthey, Heidegger and Gadamer* (Evanston, Ill.: Northwestern University Press, 1969), especially pp. 33-45, offer useful introductory surveys of a variety of ways in which the term *hermeneutics* has been employed.

[5]See Paul Ricoeur, *Interpretation Theory: Discourse and the Surplus of Meaning* (Fort Worth, Tex.: Texas Christian University Press, 1976), for an introductory discussion of some of the implications of this approach to hermeneutics. For further discussion, see Ricoeur's essays collected in *The Conflict of Interpretations: Essays in Hermeneutics,* ed. Don Ihde (Evanston, Ill.: Northwestern University

Press, 1974), and *Hermeneutics and the Human Sciences,* ed. John Thompson (Cambridge: Cambridge University Press, 1981).

[6]See especially Ricoeur's essay "What Is a Text? Explanation and Understanding," in *Hermeneutics and the Human Sciences,* pp. 145-64.

[7]Philadelphia: Fortress, 1979.

[8]Philadelphia: Fortress, 1985.

Chapter 2: Investigating Old Roads

[1]Carl E. Braaten, *History and Hermeneutics,* vol. 2 of *New Directions in Theology Today* (Philadelphia: Westminster Press, 1966), provides solid, though now somewhat dated, introductory theological discussions of the relationship. See also the essays in Robert W. Funk and Gerhard Ebeling, eds., *History and Hermeneutic, Journal for Theology and Church* Series 4 (New York: Harper, 1967).

[2]See the selected primary and secondary sources collected in section four of the bibliography, "Hermeneutics as History of Biblical Interpretation." Origen's *On First Principles,* trans. G. W. Butterworth (London: S.P.C.K., 1936), and Augustine's *On Christian Doctrine,* trans. D. W. Robertson Jr. (New York: Liberal Arts, 1958), offer classic discussions of biblical interpretation in the early church, which have exerted vast influence on later exegetes and theologians. Perhaps the most accessible introduction to this area is Robert M. Grant with David Tracy, *A Short History of the Interpretation of the Bible,* rev. ed. (Philadelphia: Fortress, 1984).

[3]Two nineteenth-century treatments which summarize this history in detail are Frederic W. Farrar, *History of Interpretation* (1886; reprint Grand Rapids, Mich.: Baker, 1961), and Milton Spenser Terry, *Biblical Hermeneutics: A Treatise on the Interpretation of the Old and New Testaments* (New York: Phillips and Hunt, 1883). For more recent extensive discussion see *The Cambridge History of the Bible,* 3 vols. (Cambridge: Cambridge University Press, 1963-1970). For a technical survey of the development of the doctrine of Scripture from the rise of medieval scholasticism to the end of the seventeenth century, see Richard A. Muller, *Post-Reformation Reformed Dogmatics,* vol. 2 of *Holy Scripture: The Cognitive Foundation of Theology* (Grand Rapids, Mich.: Baker, 1993), pp. 3-145.

[4]I have offered an assessment of this difficulty in "Allegorical Flights of Fancy: The Problem of Origen's Exegesis," *Greek Orthodox Theological Review* 32 (1987): 69-87.

[5]As evangelical scholars have wrestled with these obstacles, they have developed a variety of nuanced proposals that seek to modify and/or defend the models in light of the problems raised. See for example the essays collected in Donald McKim, ed., *A Guide to Contemporary Hermeneutics: Major Trends in Biblical Interpretation* (Grand Rapids, Mich.: Eerdmans, 1986), and in D. A. Carson and John D. Woodbridge, eds., *Hermeneutics, Authority and Canon* (Grand Rapids, Mich.: Zondervan, 1986). It is beyond the scope of this introductory work to present and discuss these more hermeneutically sophisticated approaches, especially those which rely on advanced use of literary methods (e.g., Grant R. Osborne, *The Hermeneutical*

Spiral: A Comprehensive Introduction [Downers Grove, Ill.: InterVarsity Press, 1991]) or philosophical hermeneutics (e.g., James H. Olthuis with Donald G. Bloesch, Clark H. Pinnock and Gerald T. Sheppard, *A Hermeneutics of Ultimacy: Peril or Promise?* [Lanham, Md.: University Press of America, 1987]). Rather, this chapter will present in simplified fashion two approaches to revelation as "facts" (data for propositions) and "events" (history of salvation).

[6]For further discussion of Scottish Common Sense philosophy and its influence in America see Sydney E. Ahlstrom, "The Scottish Philosophy and American Theology," *Church History* 24 (September 1955): 257-72, and Henry F. May, *The Enlightenment in America* (New York: Oxford University Press, 1976).

[7]Charles Hodge, *Systematic Theology,* 3 vols. (New York: Charles Scribner's Sons, 1872), 1:10. For Hodge's full discussion see 1:1-17.

[8]For more sophisticated, complex accounts of a propositional evangelical hermeneutics, see J. I. Packer, *"Infallible Scripture and the Role of Hermeneutics," in *Scripture and Truth,* ed. D. A. Carson and John D. Woodbridge (Grand Rapids, Mich.: Zondervan, 1983), pp. 325-56, 412-19, and the essays collected in Carson and Woodbridge, *Hermeneutics, Authority and Canon.*

[9]Josh McDowell, *Evidence That Demands a Verdict* (San Bernardino, Calif.: Here's Life, 1972), and *More Evidence That Demands a Verdict* (San Bernardino, Calif.: Here's Life, 1975).

[10]Grand Rapids, Mich.: Zondervan, 1982.

[11]R. G. Collingwood articulately develops this theme for historiography. See *The Idea of History* (Oxford: Clarendon, 1946) and *An Autobiography* (Oxford: Oxford University Press, 1939).

[12]Ludwig Wittgenstein's arguments for "meaning as use" in *Philosophische Untersuchungen/Philosophical Investigations,* trans. G. E. M. Anscombe (Oxford: Basil Blackwell, 1963), especially 1:43, have influenced contemporary philosophers of language. Wittgenstein's intriguing notion of "theology as grammar" (see 1:373) has been appropriated for Christian philosophy by Paul L. Holmer, *The Grammar of Faith* (San Francisco: Harper & Row, 1978). Hans-Georg Gadamer's use of aesthetic experience (e.g., the meanings of a work of art) in *Truth and Method,* ed. Garrett Barden and John Cumming (New York: Seabury, 1975), also points toward a more contextually dependent understanding of meaning. For a helpful commentary, see Joel Weinsheimer's *Gadamer's Hermeneutics: A Reading of "Truth and Method"* (New Haven, Conn.: Yale University Press, 1985). A more general overview of some contemporary directions in philosophy of language may be found in Paul Ricoeur, *Main Trends in Philosophy* (New York: Holmes and Meier, 1979). For a recent introduction to the application of the philosophy of language to religion, see Dan Stiver, *The Philosophy of Religious Language: Sign, Symbol and Language* (Cambridge, Mass.: Blackwell, 1995).

[13]See David C. Steinmetz's provocative article *"The Superiority of Pre-critical Exegesis," *Theology Today* 37 (1980): 27-38, for an application of this argument in the context of a challenge to the assumptions of traditional historical-critical biblical interpretation.

[14]Gadamer's development of hermeneutical consciousness in *Truth and Method* employs the concept of "horizons of meaning" to challenge a rigid historicism. See also the essays collected and translated by David Linge in Hans-Georg Gadamer, **Philosophical Hermeneutics* (Berkeley: University of California Press, 1976).

[15]Gerhard Ebeling delineates seven historical periods in the development of biblical hermeneutics in his classic German article "Hermeneutik," in *Die Religion in Geschichte und Gegenwart*, 3rd ed. (Tübingen, Germany: J. C. B. Mohr, 1959), pp. 242-64. For an English introduction see Robert M. Grant with David Tracy, *A Short History of the Interpretation of the Bible*, rev. ed. (Philadelphia: Fortress, 1984).

[16]The importance of "social location" is especially emphasized in liberation theology. See J. Severino Croatto, **Biblical Hermeneutics: Toward a Theory of Reading as the Production of Meaning*, trans. Robert R. Barr (Maryknoll, N.Y.: Orbis, 1987), and Terence J. Keegan, **Interpreting the Bible: A Popular Introduction to Biblical Hermeneutics* (New York: Paulist, 1985).

[17]Søren Kierkegaard's reflections on "The Disciple at Second Hand," in **Philosophical Fragments or A Fragment of Philosophy*, trans. David F. Swenson and Howard Hong (Princeton, N.J.: Princeton University Press, 1962), pp. 111-38, anticipate many twentieth-century concerns about our own hermeneutical assumptions.

[18]Anthony Thiselton offers detailed discussion of the significance of contemporary philosophical and literary theories of hermeneutics upon biblical interpretation in **The Two Horizons: New Testament Hermeneutics and Philosophical Description, with Special Reference to Heidegger, Bultmann, Gadamer and Wittgenstein* (Exeter, U.K.: Paternoster, 1980), and **New Horizons in Hermeneutics* (Grand Rapids, Mich.: Zondervan, 1992). See also Paul Ricoeur, **"Biblical Hermeneutics," Semeia* 4 (1975): 29-148, and **Essays on Biblical Interpretation*, ed. Lewis S. Mudge (Philadelphia: Fortress, 1980). For an application of Ricoeur's theory in the context of South American liberation theology, see Croatto, *Biblical Hermeneutics*.

[19]For recent discussion of these issues in relation to the history of Christianity see Timothy J. Wengert and Charles W. Brockwell Jr., *Telling the Churches' Stories: Ecumenical Perspectives on Writing Christian History* (Grand Rapids, Mich.: Eerdmans, 1995).

[20]Sometimes writers following the facts-of-revelation model will use the term *salvation history* to refer to the special revelation of God's saving action found in the Bible. This usage is to be distinguished from the broader usage of the history-of-salvation approach.

[21]See especially his works *Christ and Time* (Philadelphia: Westminster Press, 1951) and *Salvation in History* (London: SCM Press, 1967).

[22]G. Ernest Wright and R. H. Fuller, *The Book of the Acts of God* (Garden City, N.Y.: Doubleday/Anchor, 1960).

[23]See especially the critique of James Barr in **Old and New in Interpretation: A Study of the Two Testaments* (London: SCM Press, 1966).

[24]Paul Ricoeur's "Biblical Hermeneutics" illustrates how a theory of metaphor may be applied to parables. See also Lynn M. Poland, **Literary Criticism and Biblical Hermeneutics* (Decatur, Ga.: Scholars, 1975).

[25]See in particular Baillie's *The Idea of Revelation in Recent Thought* (London: Oxford University Press, 1956), especially pp. 50ff., which provides a clear account of revelation as the history of salvation.

[26]Ronald F. Thiemann offers an insightful description of the problem of revelation in modern theology in *Revelation and Theology: The Gospel as Narrated Promise* (Notre Dame, Ind.: University of Notre Dame Press, 1985).

[27]Immanuel Kant, *Critique of Pure Reason,* trans. J. M. D. Meiklejohn (London: George Bell and Sons, 1901). See especially "Transcendental Doctrine of the Faculty of Judgment," chap. 3, "The ground of division of all objects into Phenomena and Noumena."

[28]Kant, *Critique of Pure Reason:* "Transcendental Dialectic"; bk. 2, chap. 3, "The Ideal of Pure Reason," especially secs. 3-7.

[29]See Kierkegaard, *Philosophical Fragments,* especially the concern for a "historical point of departure" in the title-page questions. Also, cf. Gotthold Ephraim Lessing's "ugly ditch" between history and reason in "On the Proof of the Spirit and of Power," in *Lessing's Theological Writings,* trans. Henry Chadwick (Stanford, Calif.: Stanford University Press, 1957), pp. 51-56.

[30]Cf. the problems with Origen's allegorical exegesis mentioned in the introduction to this chapter.

[31]Barr, *Old and New,* pp. 65-102, especially pp. 82ff.

[32]See Thiemann, *Revelation and Theology,* p. 7. For Thiemann's development of his claims with specific theologians as examples, see pp. 9-46.

[33]Evangelical theologians who follow the facts-of-revelation route may resist the claim that their knowledge of revelation rests on an intuition of the priority of God's presence. *Intuition* (or religious insight) is a label commonly used by some conservative evangelicals to describe liberal Protestant positions. Instead, certain theologians who follow the facts-of-revelation route (e.g., the heirs to the Old Princeton tradition) would claim to rely on a commonsense realism that sees God's speaking (e.g., in Ex 14:15-18, 26) followed by an authenticating event. This view, however, still entails the assumption of the priority of God's presence through the speaking of the word from the Lord. Some sort of special category of knowing seems inevitably to be involved in the knowledge of God's revelation.

[34]For an introduction to some of the hermeneutical issues involved in the rejection of foundationalism see Paul Ricoeur, *The Conflict of Interpretations: Essays in Hermeneutics,* ed. Don Ihde (Evanston, Ill.: Northwestern University Press, 1974). Jürgen Habermas offers an introduction to these issues from the critical perspective of the Frankfurt School in *Knowledge and Human Interests,* trans. Jeremy J. Shapiro (Boston: Beacon, 1971). Also, readers of German will find Karl-Otto Apel's "hermeneutically transformed transcendental philosophy" to offer a detailed critical approach to these questions (*Transformation der Philosophie,* 2 vols. [Frankfurt: Suhrkamp, 1973]).

[35]See Gerhard Ebeling, *"The New Hermeneutics and the Early Luther," Theology Today* 21 (1964-1965): 34-46. Ebeling's perspective is based on his earlier analysis of the transition from medieval to Reformation exegesis in the development of

Luther's hermeneutics (*Evangelische Evangelienauslegung: Eine Untersuchung zu Luthers Hermeneutik* [1942; reprint Darmstadt, Germany: Wissenschaftliche Buchgesellschaft, 1962]).

[36]John Locke, *The Reasonableness of Christianity, with A Discourse of Miracles and Part of a Third Letter Concerning Toleration,* ed. I. T. Ramsey (London: Adam and Charles Black, 1958).

Chapter 3: Discovering a Better Route

[1]For example, James Sanders advocates a "canonical criticism" that utilizes existentialist hermeneutics. See James A. Sanders, *Canon and Community: A Guide to Canonical Criticism* (Philadelphia: Fortress, 1984), and **Torah and Canon* (Philadelphia: Fortress, 1972). Cf. also Sanders's location of his own view within contemporary hermeneutical discussion in James A. Sanders, ***"Hermeneutics," in *Interpreter's Dictionary of the Bible,* supp. vol., ed. Keith Crim (Nashville: Abingdon, 1976), pp. 402-7.

[2]See Albert C. Sundberg Jr., *The Old Testament of the Early Church,* Harvard Theological Studies 20 (Cambridge, Mass.: Harvard University Press, 1964). For an earlier summary of his research see Sundberg's "The Old Testament in the Early Church (A Study of Canon)," *Harvard Theological Review* 51 (1958): 205-26. For the implications of his research for the boundaries of the canon, see Albert C. Sundberg Jr., "The Protestant Old Testament Canon: Should It Be Re-examined?" *Catholic Biblical Quarterly* 28 (1966): 194-203; and "The 'Old Testament': A Christian Canon," *Catholic Biblical Quarterly* 30 (1968): 143-55. More recently Sundberg's sharp distinction between Scripture and canon has been advocated by Lee Martin McDonald in *The Formation of the Christian Biblical Canon* (Nashville: Abingdon, 1988), pp. 35-47.

[3]For example, Sundberg, presuming a negative response, raises the question "What claim does a doctrine of canon arising in Judaism following A.D. 70 have upon the doctrine of canon in the church?" ("Protestant Old Testament Canon," p. 203).

[4]Josephus, *Contra Apionem/Against Apion,* trans. H. St. J. Thackeray, Loeb Classical Library (Cambridge, Mass.: Harvard University Press, 1964), pp. 176-81.

[5]The larger context for the phrase is Ricoeur's striking remark "Beyond the desert of criticism, we wish to be called again" (Paul Ricoeur, **The Symbolism of Evil,* trans. Emerson Buchanan [Boston: Beacon, 1969], p. 349).

[6]For Childs's own description of his "change of heart" regarding Barth's hermeneutical approach, see Brevard S. Childs, "Karl Barth as Interpreter of Scripture," in *Karl Barth and the Future of Theology: A Memorial Colloquium,* ed. David L. Dickerman (New Haven, Conn.: Yale Divinity School Association, 1969), pp. 30-39, especially pp. 31-32.

[7]A more detailed examination of the relationship between Barthian hermeneutics and Childs's canonical approach may be found in my article "Canonical Hermeneutics: Childs and Barth," *Scottish Journal of Theology* 47 (1994): 61-88.

[8]Karl Barth, *Church Dogmatics,* 14 vols., trans. Geoffrey Bromiley et al. (Edinburgh: T & T Clark, 1955-1977), 1/2:722-27.

[9]"A representation based on such an examination will allow even the detailed words of the text to speak exactly as they stand" (Barth, _Church Dogmatics,_ 1/2:726).

[10]Ibid., 4/2:479.

[11]For a survey of contemporary approaches see Terence J. Keegan, *_Interpreting the Bible: A Popular Introduction to Biblical Hermeneutics_ (New York: Paulist, 1985). See also Donald McKim, ed., *_A Guide to Contemporary Hermeneutics: Major Trends in Biblical Interpretation_ (Grand Rapids, Mich.: Eerdmans, 1986), and Letty M. Russell, ed., *_Feminist Interpretation of the Bible_ (Philadelphia: Westminster Press, 1985).

[12]Barth, _Church Dogmatics,_ 1/1:120.

[13]Ibid., 1/2:473; cf. also 1/1:113.

[14]Cf. ibid., 1/1:114.

[15]Cf. Karl Barth, _The Word of God and the Word of Man,_ trans. Douglas Horton (New York: Harper & Row, 1957). For Barth's discussion of the fluidity of biblical texts, see _Church Dogmatics,_ 1/2:602.

[16]This famous slogan has been attributed to the Puritan John Robinson (c. 1575-1625).

[17]R. Alan Culpepper offers an interpretation of the Gospel of John using new literary critical approaches in *_Anatomy of the Fourth Gospel: A Study in Literary Design_ (Philadelphia: Fortress, 1983). For a theoretical analysis of reader-response criticism see Wolfgang Iser, *_The Implied Reader: Patterns of Prose Communication from Bunyan to Beckett_ (Baltimore: Johns Hopkins University Press, 1974), and *_The Act of Reading: A Theory of Aesthetic Response_ (Baltimore: Johns Hopkins University Press, 1978). See also Lynn M. Poland, *_Literary Criticism and Biblical Hermeneutics_ (Decatur, Ga.: Scholars, 1985), and further resources listed in section 3 of my bibliography, "Literary Hermeneutics."

[18]E. C. Blackman's *_Biblical Interpretation_ (Philadelphia: Westminster Press, 1957) offers a positive, moderate introduction to historical-critical exegesis. For more detailed discussion, see the essays of Rudolf Bultmann collected in *_Essays Philosophical and Theological,_ trans. J. C. G. Grieg (New York: Macmillan, 1955), especially pp. 234-61, and in *_Existence and Faith: Shorter Writings of Rudolf Bultmann,_ ed. and trans. Schubert Ogden (London: Hodder & Stoughton, 1961). Also, Bultmann's *_History and Eschatology_ (New York: Harper, 1957) spells out some of the larger theological implications of his approach.

[19]For an examination of some of these ambiguities see the discussion of "obstacles" to the facts-of-revelation route in chapter two, pp. 29-31.

[20]Brevard S. Childs, *_Introduction to the Old Testament as Scripture_ (Philadelphia: Fortress, 1979), p. 224. Childs's interpretation of Deuteronomy in a canonical context may be found on pp. 202-25. For an earlier treatment of Deuteronomy see Brevard S. Childs, "The Old Testament as Scripture of the Church," _Concordia Theological Monthly_ 43 (1972): 709-22, especially p. 720.

[21]Childs's interpretation of the book of Amos may be found in _Introduction to the Old Testament as Scripture,_ pp. 395-410.

[22]For a large-scale, detailed example of Childs's application of his canonical approach to the exegesis of a biblical book, see Brevard S. Childs, _The Book of Exodus: A_

Critical, Theological Commentary (Philadelphia: Westminster Press, 1974).

[23]Philadelphia: Fortress, 1985.

[24]Childs's interpretation of Ephesians may be found in *New Testament as Canon,* pp. 311-28.

[25]Although some Protestants may simply want to accept the sixty-six books of the traditional Protestant canon as given along with their Protestant identity, such a view ignores the diversity and universality of Scripture within the Christian community. For a Baptist perspective that argues against maintaining the traditional view, see Marvin E. Tate, "The Old Testament Apocrypha and the Old Testament Canon," *Review and Expositor* 65 (1968): 339-56.

[26]See, for example, the text-critical arguments in Kevin G. O'Connell's review of Childs's *Introduction to the Old Testament as Scripture* in *Biblical Archaeologist* 44 (1981): 187-88.

[27]Hans-Georg Gadamer, *Truth and Method,* ed. Garrett Barden and John Cumming (New York: Seabury, 1975), especially pp. 333-66. For a helpful commentary on Gadamer, see Joel C. Weinsheimer, *Gadamer's Hermeneutics: A Reading of "Truth and Method"* (New Haven, Conn.: Yale University Press, 1985).

[28]See especially Gadamer, *Truth and Method,* pp. 257-58.

[29]I have argued elsewhere that the selective appropriation of Gadamer's hermeneutical notion of tradition does not require the adoption of his philosophical framework of idealistic ontology (*Hermeneutics as Theological Prolegomena: A Canonical Approach* [Macon, Ga.: Mercer University Press, 1994], pp. 67-68).

[30]For the development of Ricoeur's theory of reading see especially the following works: *The Conflict of Interpretations: Essays in Hermeneutics,* ed. Don Ihde (Evanston, Ill.: Northwestern University Press, 1974); *The Rule of Metaphor: Multi-disciplinary Studies of the Creation of Meaning in Language,* trans. Robert Czerny (Toronto: University of Toronto Press, 1977); and *Time and Narrative,* 3 vols., trans. Kathleen (McLaughlin) Blamey and David Pellauer (Chicago: University of Chicago Press, 1984-1988).

[31]Cf. the debate on authorial intentionality between Gadamer's *Truth and Method* and E. D. Hirsch's *Validity in Interpretation* (New Haven, Conn.: Yale University Press, 1967). Cf. also the essays collected in Hans-Georg Gadamer, *Philosophical Hermeneutics,* trans. David Linge (Berkeley: University of California Press, 1976), and E. D. Hirsch, *The Art of Interpretation* (Chicago: University of Chicago Press, 1967).

[32]Anthony C. Thiselton, *New Horizons in Hermeneutics* (Grand Rapids, Mich.: Zondervan, 1992), offers a detailed analysis and evaluation of many of these new methods.

[33]Josef Bleicher, *Contemporary Hermeneutics: Hermeneutics as Method, Philosophy and Critique* (Boston: Routledge and Kegan Paul, 1980), offers an introduction to the methodological issues that underlie some recent social scientific approaches to hermeneutics, especially the critical hermeneutics of the Frankfurt School. For a complex example of the use of a sociological and literary approach to Old Testament interpretation, see Norman K. Gottwald, *The Hebrew Bible: A Socio-literary Intro-*

duction (Philadelphia: Fortress, 1985).

[34]See n. 17 and section 3 of the bibliography, "Literary Hermeneutics."

[35]See for example Childs's essay "Gerhard von Rad in American Dress," in *The Hermeneutical Quest: Essays in Honor of James Luther Mays on His Sixty-fifth Birthday* (Allison Park, Penn.: Pickwick, 1986), pp. 77-86.

[36]Feuerbach uses Hegel's philosophy in a manner that rejects Christianity and any idea of divine transcendence. See Ludwig Feuerbach, *The Essence of Christianity,* trans. George Eliot (Marian Evans) (1854; reprint New York: Harper & Row, 1957).

[37]See especially Ricoeur's essay "The Hermeneutics of Testimony," trans. David E. Stewart and Charles E. Regan, in Paul Ricoeur, *Essays on Biblical Interpretation,* ed. Lewis S. Mudge (Philadelphia: Fortress, 1980), pp. 119-54.

[38]Ricoeur is particularly referring to "Religion," chap. 7 in G. W. F. Hegel, *Phenomenology of Spirit,* trans. A. V. Miller (Oxford: Clarendon, 1977), especially pt. C, pp. 453-78.

[39]Ricoeur, "Hermeneutics of Testimony," p. 149. As Lewis Mudge explains, "The problem with Hegel's thought is that the fullness of life, of conflict, of culture, out of which the imaginative representations of the will come, is progressively swallowed up until only the concept survives. . . . Hegel's understanding of the forward progress of the will through culture is richer than Kant's, but it leads to a notion of completion of the will in 'absolute knowledge,' a metaphysical abstraction which Hegel's critics, Ricoeur among them, find pretentious and impossible" (Lewis Mudge, "Paul Ricoeur on Biblical Interpretation," in Ricoeur, *Essays on Biblical Interpretation,* pp. 1-40, at pp. 33-34).

[40]Ricoeur, "Hermeneutics of Testimony," p. 149.

[41]For a detailed example of Ricoeur's interpretation of the parables, using insights from his work on metaphor, see Paul Ricoeur, *"Biblical Hermeneutics," Semeia* 4 (1975): 29-148.

Chapter 4: Exploring the Surroundings

[1]See, for example, the essays collected in D. A. Carson and John D. Woodbridge, eds., *Hermeneutics, Authority and Canon* (Grand Rapids, Mich.: Zondervan, 1986). Also, cf. the conservative evangelical scholars included in Donald McKim, ed., *A Guide to Contemporary Hermeneutics: Major Trends in Biblical Interpretation* (Grand Rapids, Mich.: Eerdmans, 1986).

[2]Celsus attacked Christianity in his work "True Discourse." Written around C.E. 178, it is the oldest philosophical challenge to Christianity that has survived with most of its contents. Celsus's work has been preserved largely through Origen's famous refutation of it: Origen, *Contra Celsum,* trans. Henry Chadwick (Cambridge: Cambridge University Press, 1953).

[3]Porphyry (c. 232-c. 303) was a Neo-Platonic philosopher who wrote a treatise entitled "Against Christians." The work survives only in fragments found primarily in the writings of Christians who were seeking to refute it.

[4]Augustine clearly states this principle in *On Christian Doctrine,* trans. D. W.

Robertson Jr. (New York: Liberal Arts, 1958), 2.14.

[5]See Walter Bauer, *A Greek-English Lexicon of the New Testament and Other Early Christian Literature,* trans. from the 4th German ed. by William F. Arndt and F. Wilbur Gingrich (Chicago: University of Chicago Press, 1957), p. 403.

[6]Philo *Legum Allegoriae* 3.233, as cited in Bauer, *Greek-English Lexicon,* p. 403.

[7]These two periods correspond to Paul Ricoeur's distinction between the "archaeology" and the "teleology" of texts. See Paul Ricoeur, **Freud and Philosophy: An Essay in Interpretation,* trans. Denis Savage (New Haven, Conn.: Yale University Press, 1970), especially pp. 419-551, and "A Philosophical Interpretation of Freud," trans. Willis Domingo, in **The Conflict of Interpretations: Essays in Hermeneutics,* ed. Don Ihde (Evanston, Ill.: Northwestern University Press, 1974), pp. 161-76, especially pp. 173-74.

[8]See David Steinmetz's provocative article *"The Superiority of Pre-critical Exegesis," *Theology Today* 37 (1980): 27-38.

[9]See for example Georges Florovsky, *Bible, Church, Tradition: An Eastern Orthodox View,* vol. 1 in *Collected Works* (Belmont, Mass.: Nordland, 1972), especially p. 79.

[10]For competing definitions of allegory and typology see R. P. C. Hanson, **Allegory and Event: A Study of the Sources and Significance of Origen's Interpretation of Scripture* (Richmond, Va.: John Knox, 1959), and Jean Daniélou, **From Shadows to Reality: Studies in the Typology of the Fathers,* trans. Dom Wulstand Hibberd (London: Burns and Oates, 1960). For a comparison of Hanson's narrower definition of typology and broader definition of allegory with those of Daniélou, see my "Allegorical Flights of Fancy: The Problem of Origen's Exegesis," *Greek Orthodox Theological Review* 32 (1987): 69-87.

[11]Origen *Homilies on Leviticus* 3.5. For the extant text in Rufinus's translation, see Caroli Delarue and Caroli Vincente Delarue, eds., *Origenis Opera Omnia,* in *Patrologiae Cursus Completus, Series Graece,* ed. J. P. Migne (Paris, 1857), 12:429-30.

[12]For a clearly written historical introduction to Reformation biblical interpretation, see Marvin W. Anderson, *The Battle for the Gospel: The Bible and the Reformation, 1444-1589* (Grand Rapids, Mich.: Baker, 1978). I have traced some of the changing uses of the literal sense of Scripture in "The *Sensus Literalis:* A Hermeneutical Key to Biblical Exegesis," *Scottish Journal of Theology* 42 (1989): 45-65.

[13]Hans Frei's **The Eclipse of Biblical Narrative: A Study in Eighteenth and Nineteenth Century Hermeneutics* (New Haven, Conn.: Yale University Press, 1974) provides a masterfully detailed, technical study of the subject. See also the relevant chapters of Frederic Farrar, **History of Interpretation* (1886; reprint Grand Rapids, Mich.: Baker, 1961), and Robert M. Grant with David Tracy, **A Short History of the Interpretation of the Bible,* rev. ed. (Philadelphia: Fortress, 1984).

[14]For one prominent example, see Adolf von Harnack's *What Is Christianity?* trans. Thomas Bailey Saunders (New York: Harper & Brothers, 1957), especially pp. 13-15 and p. 217.

[15]See, for example, Dietrich Bonhoeffer, *Psalms: The Prayer Book of the Bible,* trans.

James H. Burtness (Minneapolis: Augsburg, 1970).

[16]For Ricoeur's use of this term, paired with "the teleology of the text," see n. 7 in this chapter.

[17]2 Corinthians 4:7 RSV.

[18]For further explanation of this terminology, borrowed from Gadamer, see the discussion of "obstacles" to the facts-of-revelation route in chapter two and the section entitled "The Hermeneutics of Tradition" in chapter three.

[19]1830; reprint Salt Lake City, Utah: Church of Jesus Christ of the Latter Day Saints, 1961.

[20]1875; reprint Boston: Trustees Under the Will of Mary Baker G. Eddy, 1934.

[21]Cf. the example of a canonical interpretation of the book of Amos discussed in chapter three.

[22]See especially Richard N. Longenecker, *Biblical Exegesis in the Apostolic Period* (Grand Rapids, Mich.: Eerdmans, 1975). See also Frederic W. Farrar, *History of Interpretation* (1886; reprint Grand Rapids, Mich.: Baker, 1961), and Milton Spenser Terry, *Biblical Hermeneutics: A Treatise on the Interpretation of the Old and New Testaments* (New York: Phillips and Hunt, 1883). For introductory overviews of the history of biblical interpretation, see Gerhard Ebeling, "Hermeneutik," in *Die Religion in Geschichte und Gegenwart*, 3rd ed. (Tübingen, Germany: J. C. B. Mohr, 1959), pp. 242-64, and Robert M. Grant with David Tracy, *A Short History of the Interpretation of the Bible*, rev. ed. (Philadelphia: Fortress, 1984). More detailed information on the history of the Bible and its interpretation may be found in *The Cambridge History of the Bible*, 3 vols. (Cambridge: Cambridge University Press, 1963-1970).

[23]For a lively theological discussion of this ancient controversy, see Arthur McGill, *Suffering: A Test of Theological Method* (Philadelphia: Westminster Press, 1968), pp. 64-82. Maurice Wiles has offered a revisionist view of the controversy, especially in his "In Defense of Arius," *Journal of Theological Studies* 13 (1962): 339-47.

[24]See Ludwig Wittgenstein's analysis of "the dawning of an aspect" in *Philosophische Untersuchungen/Philosophical Investigations*, trans. G. E. M. Anscombe (Oxford: Basil Blackwell, 1963), 2:193ff.

[25]George Lindbeck, in his pioneering work *The Nature of Doctrine: Religion and Theology in a Postliberal Age* (Philadelphia: Westminster Press, 1984), has argued for a strong emphasis on the "intratextuality" of meaning. In harmony with contemporary narrative theology, Lindbeck argues that the meaning of a text lies within the text itself. In his excursus "The Canonical Approach and the 'New Yale Theology' " (*The New Testament as Canon: An Introduction* [Philadelphia: Fortress, 1985], pp. 541-46, especially p. 545), Childs argues against this emphasis in favor of a more referential understanding of meaning. In Childs's view the Bible should be understood as "testimonies" of the "prophets and apostles" to "what God was doing in the world" (ibid.). I think an approach to hermeneutics that emphasizes the *interaction* of sense (intratextuality) and reference would offer a more balanced understanding of the meaning of Scripture.

Chapter 5: Glimpsing the Destination

[1]Cf. Karl Rahner on the dangers of separating systematic theological reflection on the one God from reflection on the doctrine of the Trinity: *The Trinity,* trans. Joseph Donceel (New York: Herder and Herder, 1970).

[2]For a brief introduction to this complex history, see J. N. D. Kelly, *Early Christian Doctrines,* 2nd ed. (New York: Harper & Row, 1960), pp. 83-137, 252-79. For more comprehensive accounts see Bertrand de Margerie, *The Christian Trinity in History,* trans. Edmund J. Fortman (Still River, Mass.: St. Bede's, 1982), and R. P. C. Hanson, *The Search for the Christian Doctrine of God: The Arian Controversy,* 318-381 (Edinburgh: T & T Clark, 1988).

[3]See Augustine *De Trinitate* 1.7, 12.6, 14.19; *St. Augustine: The Trinity,* trans. Stephen McKenna (Washington, D.C.: Catholic University of America Press, 1963), pp. 20, 348, 446-47.

[4]For a masterful philosophical discussion of the roles of "data," "warrants" and "backing" in arguments, see Stephen Toulmin, *The Uses of Argument* (Cambridge: Cambridge University Press, 1958). David Kelsey has applied Toulmin's concepts to theological arguments in *The Uses of Scripture in Recent Theology* (Philadelphia: Fortress, 1975).

[5]Karl Barth, *Church Dogmatics,* 1/1, *The Doctrine of the Word of God,* trans. G. T. Thomson (Edinburgh: T & T Clark, 1936), par. 9, "God's Three-in-Oneness," pp. 400-441, especially pp. 408-23.

[6]Rahner, *Trinity,* pp. 73-75, 103-15, especially pp. 109-15.

[7]Reginald Heber, "Holy, Holy, Holy," 1826.

[8]Ibid., from stanzas 1 and 4.

[9]This typology of approaches to doctrine is taken from George Lindbeck, *The Nature of Doctrine: Religion and Theology in a Postliberal Age* (Philadelphia: Westminster Press, 1984), especially pp. 7-12, 15-45.

[10]For Lindbeck's examples of rules, including the rule of monotheism, see ibid., pp. 92-96.

[11]Paul L. Holmer (*The Grammar of Faith* [San Francisco: Harper & Row, 1978]) applies Wittgenstein's remark about "theology as grammar" to Christian philosophical theology (Ludwig Wittgenstein, *Philosophische Untersuchungen/Philosophical Investigations,* trans. G. E. M. Anscombe [Oxford: Basil Blackwell, 1963], 1:373).

[12]In the section of chapter four entitled "The Road Markers: Biblical Authority" this theme is discussed in more detail.

[13]Cf. "παράδοξος," in H. G. Liddell, R. Scott and H. S. Jones, *A Greek-English Lexicon* (Oxford: Clarendon, 1940).

[14]Theophilus *To Autolycus* 2.15.

[15]Tertullian *Against Praxeas* 3.

[16]For a more detailed presentation of the various groups involved in the theological development of the doctrine of the Trinity, see Bernard Lonergan, *The Way to Nicea: The Dialectical Development of Trinitarian Theology,* trans. Conn O'Donovan (Philadelphia: Westminster Press, 1967).

[17]Gregory of Nyssa, *On "Not Three Gods": To Ablabius,* trans. H. A. Wilson, in *The Nicene and Post-Nicene Fathers,* ser. 2 (1892; reprint Grand Rapids, Mich.: Eerdmans, 1962), 5:331-36.

[18]Rahner, *Trinity.*

[19]Leonard Hodgson, *The Doctrine of the Trinity* (New York: Charles Scribner's Sons, 1944).

[20]Jürgen Moltmann, *The Trinity and the Kingdom: The Doctrine of God,* trans. Margaret Kohl (San Francisco: Harper & Row, 1981).

[21]Schubert M. Ogden, *The Reality of God and Other Essays* (New York: Harper & Row, 1977).

[22]See, for example, John B. Cobb Jr., *God and the World* (Philadelphia: Westminster Press, 1969).

[23]Alfred North Whitehead, *Process and Reality: An Essay in Cosmology* (New York: Macmillan, 1929). For an explicit application see John B. Cobb Jr., *A Christian Natural Theology: Based on the Thought of Alfred North Whitehead* (Philadelphia: Westminster Press, 1966).

[24]Cf. Lindbeck, *Nature of Doctrine,* especially pp. 104-5.

[25]For a chronicling of the demise of the Biblical Theology movement, see Brevard S. Childs, *Biblical Theology in Crisis* (Philadelphia: Westminster Press, 1970).

[26]See especially Emil Brunner, *Truth as Encounter,* trans. Amandus W. Loos and David Cairns (Philadelphia: Westminster Press, 1964).

[27]Moltmann, *Trinity and the Kingdom.* See also Jürgen Moltmann, *Theology of Hope: On the Grounds and Implications of a Christian Eschatology,* trans. James W. Leitch (New York: Harper & Row, 1967), and *The Crucified God,* trans. R. A. Wilson and John Bowden (New York: Harper & Row, 1974).

[28]See for example Eberhard Jüngel, *God as the Mystery of the World: On the Foundation of the Theology of the Crucified One in the Dispute Between Theism and Atheism,* trans. Darrell L. Guder (Grand Rapids, Mich.: Eerdmans, 1983).

[29]Cf. the psalms of complaint or lament found across the Psalter. As mentioned in the previous section, Psalm 22:1, which Jesus cries out upon the cross (Mt 27:46; Mk 15:34), is perhaps the best-known example.

[30]For a spirited introduction to some contemporary responses to the problem, see Stephen T. Davis, ed., *Encountering Evil: Live Options in Theodicy* (Atlanta: John Knox, 1981).

[31]Harold S. Kushner, *When Bad Things Happen to Good People* (New York: Avon, 1981).

[32]See, for instance, John Cobb's process theodicy in *God and the World.* For a balanced assessment of the contributions of process theology to the theodicy issue, see Paul S. Fiddes, *The Creative Suffering of God* (Oxford: Clarendon, 1988).

[33]See Augustine's images and discussion of the relations between the persons of the Trinity in *De Trinitate.*

[34]Moltmann, *Crucified God.* See also Moltmann's "God and Suffering," in *Trinity and the Kingdom,* pp. 47-52. For a helpful discussion of the limitations of this view, see John J. O'Donnell, *Trinity and Temporality: The Christian Doctrine of God in*

the Light of Process Theology and the Theology of Hope (Oxford: Oxford University Press, 1983), especially pp. 147-56. Fiddes, *Creative Suffering,* also offers valuable insight into the strengths and weaknesses of Moltmann's view.

[35]I have offered some historical background and further development of this theme in "Lex Cantandi, Lex Credendi: Theology and Hymnody," in *Learning from Beauty: W. L. Hendricks Festschrift* (Macon, Ga.: Mercer University Press, forthcoming).

[36]Reginald Heber, "Holy, Holy, Holy," 1826, stanza 1.

Bibliography

During the last three decades of the twentieth century, theological hermeneutics has undergone a paradigm shift. Hermeneutics may no longer be seen as an isolated methodological discipline of primary concern to philologists and historians. Rather, contemporary theological hermeneutics is a multicultural, cross-disciplinary endeavor at the forefront of much current scholarship in the humanities and social sciences. How can the beginning student approaching this exploding field for the first time get a perspective on its scope and significance to guide his or her research? This bibliography represents an attempt to respond to this commonly perceived need.

The following list is *not* intended as a comprehensive bibliography of the field. Entries are restricted to books and articles written or translated into English. More specialized bibliographies already exist, and some may be found listed in the first section of this work. Instead, this bibliography seeks to offer a highly selective introduction to and construal of theological hermeneutics to assist teachers, students and others beginning research in this significant area.

An asterisk (*) appearing before titles listed in the notes to the book indicates that they may be found with further annotation among the entries in this bibliography.

I. Bibliographies on Hermeneutics

"Bibliographical Guide to Hermeneutics and Critical Theory." *Cultural Hermeneutics* 2 (1975): 379-90.

Bleicher, Josef. *Contemporary Hermeneutics: Hermeneutics as Method, Philosophy and Critique.* Boston: Routledge and Kegan Paul, 1980, pp. 272-80. Especially helpful with the "critical hermeneutics" of the Frankfurt School.

"A Brief Checklist of Important Titles in Hermeneutics." *Journal of Religion* 55 (1975): 371-74. Annotated introductory bibliography. The entire issue of the journal (pp. 295-370) is devoted to hermeneutics.

Childs, Brevard S. *Introduction to the Old Testament as Scripture.* Philadelphia: Fortress, 1979, pp. 46-49, 69-71, 84-88, 659-60. Bibliography on the problem of canon from the perspective of Old Testament hermeneutics.

_____. *The New Testament as Canon: An Introduction.* Philadelphia: Fortress, 1985, pp. 3-5, 16-18, 34-35, 518-21. Bibliography on the problem of canon from the perspective of New Testament hermeneutics.

Culpepper, R. Alan. *Anatomy of the Fourth Gospel: A Study in Literary Design.* Philadelphia: Fortress, 1983, pp. 239-48. Contemporary literary critical materials relating to biblical interpretation.

Dornisch, Loretta. "Paul Ricoeur and Biblical Interpretation: A Selected Bibliography." *Semeia* 4 (1975): pp. 23-26. The entire issue of the journal is devoted to Ricoeur.

Farrar, Frederic W. *History of Interpretation.* London: Macmillan, 1886; reprint Grand Rapids, Mich.: Baker Book House, 1961, pp. 479-91. Extensive nineteenth-century bibliography on history of exegesis. Special focus on patristic methods of interpretation.

Howard, Roy J. *Three Faces of Hermeneutics: An Introduction to Current Theories of Understanding.* Berkeley: University of California Press, 1982, pp. 177-84. Introductory bibliography for phenomenological and critical hermeneutics.

Palmer, Richard E. *Hermeneutics: Interpretation Theory in Schleiermacher, Dilthey, Heidegger and Gadamer.* Evanston, Ill.: Northwestern University Press, 1969, pp. 254-74. Strength in nineteenth- and twentieth-century German hermeneutical philosophy.

Thiselton, Anthony C. *New Horizons in Hermeneutics.* Grand Rapids, Mich.: Zondervan, 1992, pp. 621-61. Diverse selection of theoretical models of reading and interpretation which impact biblical hermeneutics. Specially designated "key primary sources for modern hermeneutical theory."

_____. *The Two Horizons: New Testament Hermeneutics and Philosophical Description with Special Reference to Heidegger, Bultmann, Gadamer and Wittgenstein.* Exeter, U.K.: Paternoster, 1980, pp. 447-66. Extensive bibliography on philosophy of language; wide-ranging selection of New Testament studies and contemporary theology.

Thompson, John B. "Select Bibliography." In *Critical Hermeneutics: A Study in the Thought of Paul Ricoeur and Jürgen Habermas.* London: Cambridge University Press, 1982, pp. 241-51. Focuses on philosophy of social science, with particular attention to ordinary language philosophy, as well as hermeneutic phenomenology and critical theory.

II. Philosophical and Theological Hermeneutics

A. Aesthetical

Bouma-Prediger, Steve. "Rorty's Pragmatism and Gadamer's Hermeneutics." *Journal of the American Academy of Religion* 57 (1982): 313-24. Rorty quite selectively borrows from Gadamer, disguising the differences between them.

Bourgeois, Patrick L. *Extension of Ricoeur's Hermeneutic.* The Hague: Martinus Nijhoff, 1975. Interpretation of Ricoeur's hermeneutic in light of his earlier philosophy of will.

Bozarth-Campbell, Alla. *The Word's Body: An Incarnational Aesthetic of Interpreta-*

tion. Tuscaloosa: University of Alabama Press, 1979. Philosophical analysis of interpretation of literature as "performance," utilizing a hermeneutical aesthetic.

Cassirer, Ernst. *The Philosophy of Symbolic Forms.* 3 vols. Trans. Ralph Mannheim. New Haven, Conn.: Yale University Press, 1953-1957. "Philosophical anthropology" based on the "symbolic forms of culture." Cassirer's "aesthetic symbols" are especially important for later philosophers like Langer and Ricoeur.

Derrida, Jacques. *Speech and Phenomena, and Other Essays on Husserl's Theory of Signs.* Trans. David B. Allison. Evanston, Ill.: Northwestern University Press, 1973. Derrida's critique of Husserl. Discussion of deconstruction in "The Voice That Keeps Silent," pp. 70-87. Also see especially "Form and Meaning: A Note on the Phenomenology of Language," pp. 107-28.

Gadamer, Hans-Georg. *Philosophical Hermeneutics.* Trans. David Linge. Berkeley: University of California Press, 1976. Note Linge's extensive introduction. Essays chosen for translation are primarily later writings on themes related to *Truth and Method.*

_____. *Truth and Method.* Ed. Garrett Barden and John Cumming. New York: Seabury, 1975. Uses aesthetic experience to develop a new hermeneutical consciousness that transcends historicism.

Ihde, Don. *Hermeneutic Phenomenology: The Philosophy of Paul Ricoeur.* Evanston, Ill.: Northwestern University Press, 1971. Analysis of Ricoeur's philosophy from the hermeneutical perspective developed in his writings in the 1960s.

Panikkar, Raimundo. *Myth, Faith and Hermeneutics: Cross-Cultural Studies.* New York: Paulist, 1979. Collection of essays reflecting Panikkar's Hindu-Christian metatheology. Section on hermeneutics, pp. 322-460.

Ricoeur, Paul. *The Conflict of Interpretations: Essays in Hermeneutics.* Ed. Don Ihde. Evanston, Ill.: Northwestern University Press, 1974. Essays written from 1960 to 1969 on the relation of hermeneutics to structuralism, psychoanalysis, phenomenology and religion.

_____. *Freud and Philosophy: An Essay on Interpretation.* Trans. Denis Savage. New Haven, Conn.: Yale University Press, 1970. Hermeneutics as "demystification" ("suspicion") versus hermeneutics as "demythologizing." Psychoanalysis as a form of hermeneutics.

_____. *Hermeneutics and the Human Sciences.* Ed. John Thompson. Cambridge: Cambridge University Press, 1981. Collected essays on hermeneutics from the 1970s.

_____. *Interpretation Theory: Discourse and the Surplus of Meaning.* Fort Worth, Tex.: Texas Christian University Press, 1976. Discusses the meaning of language as a "work." Develops notion of "plurivocity" of textual meaning.

_____. *The Rule of Metaphor: Multi-disciplinary Studies of the Creation of Meaning in Language.* Trans. Robert Czerny. Toronto: University of Toronto Press, 1977. Philosophical examination of metaphor from Aristotle to contemporary philosophy. Traces a path "which begins with classical rhetoric, passes through semiotics and semantics, and finally reaches hermeneutics."

_____. *The Symbolism of Evil.* Trans. Emerson Buchanan. Boston: Beacon, 1969.

Signals methodological shift from earlier descriptive phenomenology toward hermeneutics. Utilizes "phenomenology of confession" to analyze meaning of myths.

_____. *Time and Narrative.* 3 vols. Trans. Kathleen (McLaughlin) Blamey and David Pellauer. Chicago: University of Chicago Press, 1984-1988. Extension of *The Rule of Metaphor* to analyze the creation of meaning at the level of text.

Schwartz, Sanford. "Hermeneutics and the Productive Imagination: Paul Ricoeur in the 1970s." *Journal of Religion* 63 (1983): 290-300. Analysis of development of Ricoeur's "hermeneutical arc" from his studies in textuality.

Weinsheimer, Joel C. *Gadamer's Hermeneutics: A Reading of "Truth and Method."* New Haven, Conn.: Yale University Press, 1985. Section-by-section commentary.

Winquist, Charles E. *Homecoming: Interpretation, Transformation and Individuation.* Missoula, Mont.: Scholars, 1978. "Homecoming" as the point of convergence between Jungian psychology and philosophical phenomenology. Significant use of contemporary literary sources.

B. Theological

Baillie, John. *The Idea of Revelation in Recent Thought.* London: Oxford University Press, 1956. Classic exposition of history of salvation model.

Braaten, Carl E. *History and Hermeneutics.* New Directions in Theology Today 2. Philadelphia: Westminster Press, 1966. Examines the relationship between revelation and history, with special attention to Pannenberg.

Dulles, Avery. "Hermeneutical Theology." *Communio* 6 (1979): 16-37. Evaluation of theological strengths and weaknesses of post-Heideggerian "hermeneutical theology." Christian theology must critique Heideggerian phenomenology.

Ebeling, Gerhard. *Word and Faith.* Trans. James W. Leitch. Philadelphia: Fortress, 1963. "Word-event theology." See especially the essay "Word of God and Hermeneutics," pp. 305-32.

Fiorenza, Francis Schüssler. *Foundational Theology: Jesus and the Church.* New York: Crossroad, 1984. Utilizes a "reconstructive hermeneutic" to interpret foundational theology.

Fox-Genovese, Elizabeth. "For Feminist Interpretation." *Union Seminary Quarterly Review* 35 (1979-80): 5-14. Theory of interpretation as the "intellectual foundation" of a feminist hermeneutics that "restores subjective pluralism."

Frei, Hans W. *The Identity of Jesus Christ: The Hermeneutical Bases of Dogmatic Theology.* Philadelphia: Fortress, 1975. Reading of Gospels as realistic narratives that render the identity of Jesus Christ; argues that in Jesus Christ identity and presence are given together.

Funk, Robert W. *Language, Hermeneutic and the Word of God.* New York: Harper, 1966. Phenomenological approach with special attention to New Testament issues.

Funk, Robert W., and Gerhard Ebeling, eds. *History and Hermeneutic. Journal for Theology and the Church* Series 4. New York: Harper, 1967. Articles by Bultmann, Gogarten, Kimmerle, Pannenberg, Rendtorff, Steiger and Zimmerli.

Goldingay, John E. "The Hermeneutics of Liberation Theology." *Horizons of Biblical*

Theology 4-5 (1982-1983): 133-61. Critical evaluation of the hermeneutics of a variety of black and Latin American liberation theologians.

Herzog, Frederick. *Understanding God: The Key Issue in Present-Day Protestant Thought.* New York: Charles Scribner's Sons, 1966. Examines "historico-ontological hermeneutic" in Gospel of John and "new hermeneutic movement." Argues for a trinitarian "hermeneutic of God" rather than a "hermeneutic of faith."

Holmer, Paul L. *The Grammar of Faith.* San Francisco: Harper & Row, 1978. Combines insights from Wittgenstein and Kierkegaard in an attempt to understand Christian piety.

Hopper, Stanley R., and David L. Miller, eds. *Interpretation: The Poetry of Meaning.* New York: Harcourt, Brace and World, 1967. Papers from 1966 Consultation on Hermeneutics at Drew University. Note especially Heinrich Ott's paper, "Hermeneutics and Personhood," pp. 14-33.

Jeanrond, Werner G. *Theological Hermeneutics: Development and Significance.* New York: Crossroad, 1991. Traces historical development and argues for an "ethics of reading" related to Christian identity.

Kelsey, David H. *The Uses of Scripture in Recent Theology.* Philadelphia: Fortress, 1975. Utilizes Stephen Toulmin's analysis of arguments to describe the various ways theologians use Scripture.

Kierkegaard, Søren. *Philosophical Fragments: Or, A Fragment of Philosophy.* Trans. David F. Swenson and Howard Hong. Princeton, N.J.: Princeton University Press, 1962. See especially "The Disciple at Second Hand," pp. 111-38.

Lessing, Gotthold E. *Lessing's Theological Writings.* Trans. Henry Chadwick. Stanford, Calif.: Stanford University Press, 1957. Rationalist approach of the Enlightenment. See especially "On the Proof of the Spirit and of Power," pp. 51-56. Also note Chadwick's introductory essay, pp. 9-49.

Lindbeck, George. *The Nature of Doctrine: Religion and Theology in a Postliberal Age.* Philadelphia: Westminster Press, 1984. Advocates a "cultural-linguistic" approach to doctrine, as distinguished from "cognitive-propositional" and "experiential-expressive" approaches. Doctrines are "instantiations of rules" which are authoritative for religious communities.

Lundin, Roger, Anthony C. Thiselton and Clarence Walhout. *The Responsibility of Hermeneutics.* Grand Rapids, Mich.: Eerdmans, 1985. Asserts "the exhaustion of our traditional interpretive models" and argues for an understanding of textual meaning as performance.

Marlé, René. *Introduction to Hermeneutics.* Trans. E. Froment and R. Albrecht. New York: Herder and Herder, 1967. Special attention to neo-orthodox and existential interpretation and the implications of modern hermeneutics for Catholic theology.

Muller, Richard A. *The Study of Theology: From Biblical Interpretation to Contemporary Formulation.* Foundations of Contemporary Interpretation 7. Grand Rapids, Mich.: Zondervan, 1991. Seeks to locate hermeneutics systematically within the theological disciplines and to integrate hermeneutics and practical theology.

Ommen, Thomas B. *The Hermeneutics of Dogma.* Missoula, Mont.: Scholars, 1975. Attempts to formulate a hermeneutic for Catholic dogma in light of the New

Hermeneutic and Gadamer.

Pannenberg, Wolfhart. "Hermeneutics and Universal History." *History and Herme-neutic.* Ed. Robert W. Funk and Gerhard Ebeling. New York: Harper, 1967, pp. 122-52. Argues against the New Hermeneutic and Gadamer.

Robinson, James M., and John B. Cobb Jr., eds. *The Later Heidegger and Theology.* New York: Harper, 1963. Summarizes German discussion of role of language in later Heidegger and its implications for systematic theology (especially the views of Heinrich Ott). American response and evaluation by Come, Michalson, Ogden and Cobb.

_____. *The New Hermeneutic.* New York: Harper, 1964. Papers from 1962 Consult-ation on Hermeneutics at Drew University, with extensive introduction by Robin-son (pp. 1-77). American responses to work of Ebeling and Fuchs.

Schillebeeckx, Edward. *The Understanding of Faith: Interpretation and Criticism.* Trans. N. D. Smith. London: Sheed and Ward, 1974. Attempts to reconstruct theological hermeneutics in light of the rise of critical hermeneutics (especially Habermas) and to incorporate praxis into theological reflection.

Schleiermacher, Friedrich. *Hermeneutics: The Handwritten Manuscripts.* Trans. James Duke and Jack Forstman. Missoula, Mont.: Scholars, 1977. Hermeneutics as "the art of understanding"; Romantic hermeneutics—reconstructing and reex-periencing the mind of the author.

Stroup, George W. *The Promise of Narrative Theology: Recovering the Gospel in the Church.* Atlanta: John Knox, 1981. See especially "The Hermeneutics of Christian Narrative," pp. 199-261.

Thiemann, Ronald F. *Revelation and Theology: The Gospel as Narrated Promise.* Notre Dame, Ind.: University of Notre Dame Press, 1985. Describes impasse of doctrine of revelation in modern theology and offers a narrative response.

Winquist, Charles E. *Practical Hermeneutics: A Revised Agenda for Ministry.* Mis-soula, Mont.: Scholars, 1980. Minister as one who experiences conversion to a new vision of life and assists others to do the same; pastoral care as "interpretive analysis" of life stories.

_____. *The Transcendental Imagination: An Essay in Philosophical Theology.* The Hague: Nijhoff, 1972. Argues for the "intellectuality" of transcendental imagina-tion (Whitehead); offers condensed and controversial critique of Kant, Lonergan and Heidegger. Explores implications for theological hermeneutics.

Wood, Charles M. "The Task of Theological Hermeneutics." *Perkins School of Theology Journal* 33 (1980): 1-8. Theological hermeneutics as "Christian under-standing of Christian texts."

Wood, Laurence E. "History and Hermeneutics: A Pannenbergian Perspective." *Wesleyan Theological Journal* 16 (1981): 7-22. Defends Pannenberg's view of the positive relationship between history and faith: "neo-Hegelian epistemology" is allied with faith against the Kantian fact-value dichotomy.

C. Critical (Psychosocial)

Habermas, Jürgen. "The Hermeneutic Claim to Universality." Trans. Josef Bleicher.

In Josef Bleicher, *Contemporary Hermeneutics: Hermeneutics as Method, Philosophy and Critique*. Boston: Routledge and Kegan Paul, 1980, pp. 181-211. Argues contra Gadamer for limits on hermeneutical understanding via the "scenic understanding" of psychoanalysis.

_____. *Knowledge and Human Interests*. Trans. Jeremy J. Shapiro. Boston: Beacon, 1971. By "analyzing the connections between knowledge and human interests" through a reconstruction of the "dissolution of epistemology" beginning with Hegel's critique of Kant and ending in modern positivism, Habermas seeks to demonstrate that "a radical critique of knowledge is possible only as social theory." Psychoanalysis serves as a model of such critique. Also note especially "Dilthey's Theory of Understanding Expression."

_____. *Theory and Practice*. London: Heinemann, 1974. Argues for model of "emancipatory praxis" based on critique of ideology.

Hekman, Susan J. *Hermeneutics and the Sociology of Knowledge*. Notre Dame, Ind.: University of Notre Dame Press, 1986. Seeks to develop a theological synthesis between the work of Mannheim and that of Gadamer.

Held, David. *Introduction to Critical Theory: Horkheimer to Habermas*. London: Hutchinson, 1980.

Thompson, John B. *Critical Hermeneutics: A Study in the Thought of Paul Ricoeur and Jürgen Habermas*. Cambridge: Cambridge University Press, 1981. Philosophy of social science exposition and critique of Wittgenstein, Ricoeur and Habermas. Proposes an epistemological foundation for "a critical theory of the interpretation of action."

D. General

Allen, Douglas. *Structure and Creativity in Religion: Hermeneutics in Mircea Eliade's Phenomenology and New Directions*. New York: Mouton, 1978. Describes Eliade's phenomenological approach to religion as founded on a contemporary "hermeneutical framework."

Aristotle. *Peri Hermeneias (De Interpretatione)*. In *Aristotle: The Basic Works*. Ed. Richard McKeon. New York: Random House, 1941, pp. 40-61. Interpretation as "enunciation."

Beardslee, William A. "Recent Hermeneutics and Process Thought." *Process Studies* 12 (1982): 65-76. Describes how process thought can lead to an understanding of the relationship between narrative and a meaningful world of actual occurrences, through a hermeneutic of self-creation.

Betti, Emilio. "Hermeneutics as the General Methodology of the *Geisteswissenschaften*." Trans. Josef Bleicher. In Josef Bleicher, *Contemporary Hermeneutics: Hermeneutics as Method, Philosophy and Critique*. Boston: Routledge and Kegan Paul, 1980, pp. 51-94. Argues for historical objectivity in interpretation, polemicizing against Bultmann, Ebeling and Gadamer.

Bleicher, Josef. *Contemporary Hermeneutics: Hermeneutics as Method, Philosophy and Critique*. Boston: Routledge and Kegan Paul, 1980. Surveys modern hermeneutics from Betti through early Ricoeur from a sociological perspective. Emphasis on Frankfurt School, especially Habermas.

_____. *The Hermeneutic Imagination.* Boston: Routledge and Kegan Paul, 1982.

Brenneman, Walter L., Stanley O. Yarian and Alan M. Olson. *The Seeing Eye: Hermeneutical Phenomenology in the Study of Religion.* University Park: Pennsylvania State University Press, 1982. Seeks to link phenomenological hermeneutics with the phenomenological approach to religion (Eliade).

Collingwood, R. G. *An Autobiography.* Oxford: Oxford University Press, 1939. Historical understanding as reconstruction of the "questions" that historical actions "answer"; parallels Gadamer's view of dialogue.

_____. *The Idea of History.* Oxford: Clarendon, 1946. Argues for necessity of historical subjectivity.

Dilthey, Wilhelm. "The Development of Hermeneutics." In Wilhelm Dilthey, *Selected Writings.* Ed. and trans. H. P. Rickman. Cambridge: Cambridge University Press, 1976, pp. 246-63. Hermeneutics as a problem of historical understanding and a method for seeking "objectively valid" interpretations of "expressions of lived experience." Concludes with description of Schleiermacher's hermeneutics.

Hanson, Bo. *Application of Rules in New Situations: A Hermeneutical Study.* Lund, Sweden: CWK Gleerup, 1977. Philosophical treatment of the question of obedience in interpretation from a hermeneutical perspective.

Heidegger, Martin. *Being and Time.* Trans. John Macquarrie and Edward Robinson. London: SCM Press, 1962. Heidegger's temporal analytic of *Dasein* provides the ontological basis for hermeneutic phenomenology. Heidegger characterizes his project here as a "hermeneutic of *Dasein.*"

_____. *On the Way to Language.* Trans. Peter D. Hertz. New York: Harper & Row, 1971. Essays of later Heidegger, reflecting the linguistic "turn" of his existential ontology.

Hollinger, Robert, ed. *Hermeneutics and Praxis.* Notre Dame, Ind.: University of Notre Dame Press, 1985. Collection of philosophical essays focusing on Heidegger, Gadamer and Richard Rorty.

Howard, Roy J. *Three Faces of Hermeneutics: An Introduction to Current Theories of Understanding.* Berkeley: University of California Press, 1982. Philosophical hermeneutics as analytic (Wittgenstein), psychosocial (Habermas) and ontological (Gadamer).

Palmer, Richard E. *Hermeneutics: Interpretation Theory in Schleiermacher, Dilthey, Heidegger and Gadamer.* Evanston, Ill.: Northwestern University Press, 1969. Introduction to the development of philosophical hermeneutics from a phenomenological perspective; implications for literary interpretation.

_____. "Towards a Post-modern Interpretive Self-Awareness." *Journal of Religion* 55 (1975): 313-26. Interaction of hermeneutics and modern philosophy. Special attention to Nietzsche's contribution to the revision of hermeneutics.

Peters, Ted. "Trust in History: Gadamer's Hermeneutics and Pannenberg's Apologetic Method." *Journal of Religion* 55 (1975): 36-56. Pannenberg's utilization and extension of hermeneutics in the service of apologetics.

Raschke, Carl A. *The Alchemy of the Word: Language and the End of Theology.*

Missoula, Mont.: Scholars, 1979. Implications of later Heidegger for modern interpretation. Argues for move "from theology to dialogy."

Ricoeur, Paul. *Fallible Man: Philosophy of the Will.* Trans. Charles Kelbley. Rev. ed. Bronx, N.Y.: Fordham University Press, 1985. Ricoeur's second work in philosophical anthropology (following *Freedom and Nature*). Descriptive phenomenology.

_____. *Freedom and Nature: The Voluntary and the Involuntary.* Trans. E. B. Kohak. Evanston, Ill.: Northwestern University Press, 1966. Ricoeur's first work on the "philosophy of the will" (1950). Application of phenomenology to philosophical anthropology.

_____. *History and Truth.* Trans. Charles A. Kelbley. Evanston, Ill.: Northwestern University Press, 1965. Early essays on significance of historical work and philosophical "critique of civilization."

_____. *Husserl: An Analysis of His Phenomenology.* Trans. Edward G. Ballard and Lester Embree. Evanston, Ill.: Northwestern University Press, 1967. Essays interpreting Husserl's major works, developing out of Ricoeur's work as a translator of Husserl's writings and an historian of phenomenology.

_____. *Main Trends in Philosophy.* New York: Holmes and Meier, 1979. Assisted by specialists, Ricoeur synthesizes theoretical issues and summarizes current discussion for each of the major subfields of contemporary philosophical research.

_____. *Political and Social Essays.* Ed. David Stewart and Joseph Bien. Athens: Ohio University Press, 1974. Utilizes "a method of approximation and convergence" to discuss contemporary political and social issues.

Seung, T. K. *Structuralism and Hermeneutics.* New York: Columbia University Press, 1982. Critiques classical structuralism (Lévi-Strauss) and "poststructuralism" (Derrida).

Shapiro, Gary, and Alan Sica, eds. *Hermeneutics: Questions and Prospects.* Amherst: University of Massachusetts Press, 1984. Anthology of essays on contemporary hermeneutics in philosophy, literature and social sciences.

Thulstrup, Niels. "An Observation Concerning Past and Present Hermeneutics." *Orbis Litterarum* 22 (1967): 24-44. Discusses contrast between Betti and Gadamer.

Toulmin, Stephen. *The Uses of Argument.* Cambridge: Cambridge University Press, 1958. Jurisprudence rather than mathematics as model for analyzing logical procedures of arguments. Data, warrants and backing as pattern of arguments.

Wittgenstein, Ludwig. *Philosophische Untersuchungen/Philosophical Investigations.* Trans. G. E. M. Anscombe. Oxford: Basil Blackwell, 1963. Philosophy of language which emphasizes "meaning as use" and "forms of life" and challenges foundationalist approaches.

Wood, Charles Monroe. *Theory of Religious Understanding: A Critique of the Hermeneutics of Joachim Wach.* Missoula, Mont.: Scholars, 1975. Utilizes Wittgenstein to offer a critique of Wach.

III. Literary Hermeneutics

Auerbach, Erich. *Mimesis: The Representation of Reality in Western Literature.* Trans. Willard R. Trask. Princeton. N.J.: Princeton University Press, 1953. Traces "the interpretation of reality through literary representation of 'imitation' " across the history of Western culture. Note especially the brilliant interpretation of Abraham's sacrifice of Isaac within the essay "Odysseus' Scar," pp. 3-23.

Barthes, Roland. *Elements of Semiology.* Trans. Annette Lavers and Colin Smith. New York: Hill and Wang, 1977. Structuralist literary theory.

Booth, Wayne C. *The Rhetoric of Fiction.* Chicago: University of Chicago Press, 1961. Develops concepts of "implied author" and "implied reader."

_____. *A Rhetoric of Irony.* Chicago: University of Chicago Press, 1974. Irony as a central literary device for moving between levels of meaning.

Chatman, Seymour. *Story and Discourse: Narrative Structure in Fiction and Film.* Ithaca, N.Y.: Cornell University Press, 1978. Comprehensive approach to contemporary narrative theory. "Story" is "the content element of narrative," and "discourse" is "the formal element."

Culler, Jonathan. *Structuralist Poetics: Structuralism, Linguistics and the Study of Literature.* Ithaca, N.Y.: Cornell University Press, 1975. Summarizes, systematizes and criticizes contemporary structuralism in its application to literature.

Eco, Umberto. *The Role of the Reader: Explorations in the Semiotics of Texts.* Bloomington: Indiana University Press, 1975. Readers are active interpreters who are part of the "creation" of texts. "Open texts" versus "closed texts."

Frye, Northrop. *Anatomy of Criticism: Four Essays.* Princeton, N.J.: Princeton University Press, 1957. Literary criticism as historical (modes), ethical (symbols), archetypal (myths) and theoretical (genres).

_____. *The Great Code: The Bible and Literature.* New York: Harcourt Brace Jovanovich, 1982. Argues for unity of Bible through recurrent mythological imagery. "Double mirror" pattern.

Hirsch, E. D. *The Art of Interpretation.* Chicago: University of Chicago Press, 1967. Essays and lectures on current issues in interpretation and the "valuative dimension."

_____. *Validity in Interpretation.* New Haven, Conn.: Yale University Press, 1967. Hermeneutics as foundational for all literary interpretation. Argues for author's intentionality as norm of valid interpretation. See especially his critique of Gadamer, pp. 245-64, which originally appeared as "Gadamer's Theory of Interpretation," *Review of Metaphysics* 18 (1965): 488-507.

Hoy, David Couzens. *The Critical Circle: Literature, History and Philosophical Hermeneutics.* Berkeley: University of California Press, 1978. Impact of Gadamer's philosophical hermeneutics on literary criticism. Can Gadamer's "critique of objectivism" avoid "falling into relativism"?

Ingarden, Roman. *The Cognition of the Literary Work of Art.* Trans. R. A. Crowley and K. R. Olson. Evanston, Ill.: Northwestern University Press, 1973. Phenomenological approach to literary criticism.

Iser, Wolfgang. *The Act of Reading: A Theory of Aesthetic Response.* Baltimore: Johns Hopkins University Press, 1978. Dialectical analysis of the reading process.

_____. *The Implied Reader: Patterns of Communication in Prose Fiction from Bunyan to Beckett.* Baltimore: Johns Hopkins University Press, 1974. Expands notion of implied reader to include not only the presupposed audience but also the reader's actualization of the structures of the narrative text.

Jauss, Hans Robert. *Aesthetic Experience and Literary Hermeneutics.* Trans. Michael Shaw. Minneapolis: University of Minnesota Press, 1982. "Double task" of hermeneutics: reconstruction of history of interpretation and clarification of process of meaning for current reader. Aesthetic enjoyment as "dialectic" between self-enjoyment and other-enjoyment.

_____. "Limits and Tasks of Literary Hermeneutics." *Diogenes* 17 (1980): 92-119.

_____. *Toward an Aesthetic of Reception.* Trans. Timothy Bahti. Minneapolis: University of Minnesota Press, 1982. Jauss's "reception theory" offers a theoretical foundation for much modern reader-response criticism.

Juhl, P. D. *Interpretation: An Essay in the Philosophy of Literary Criticism.* Princeton, N.J.: Princeton University Press, 1980. Offers an analysis of "our common concept of the meaning of a literary work" and argues for "one and only one correct interpretation" (cf. Hirsch).

Kermode, J. Frank. *The Genesis of Secrecy: On the Interpretation of Narrative.* Cambridge, Mass.: Harvard University Press, 1979. Examination of the Gospels as literary narratives exemplifying the problems of interpretation, especially "opacity" and the distinguishing of possible meanings from the central meaning of the narrative.

Krieger, Murray. *A Window to Criticism: Shakespeare's Sonnets and Modern Poetics.* Princeton, N.J.: Princeton University Press, 1964. Seeks to find a way beyond the limitations on meaning found in the New Criticism.

Mazzeo, Joseph Anthony. *Varieties of Interpretation.* Notre Dame, Ind.: University of Notre Dame Press, 1978. Essays illustrating "recurrent and crucial occasions in cultural history" which "demand" interpretation.

Palmer, Richard E. "Postmodern Hermeneutics and the Act of Reading." *Notre Dame English Journal: A Journal of Religion in Literature* 15 (1983): 55-84. Critique of reader-response criticism as not postmodern, but rather a retreat into subjectivism. Gadamer and Ricoeur represent "positive postmodern hermeneutics"; Derrida, Foucault and the Yale critics represent "negative postmodern hermeneutics."

Scholes, Robert, and Robert Kellogg. *The Nature of Narrative.* New York: Oxford University Press, 1966. Argues for a broad view of narrative ("story and storyteller") in Western literary tradition. See especially chap. 4, "Meaning in Narrative," pp. 82-159.

Uspensky, Boris. *A Poetics of Composition: The Structure of the Artistic Text and Typology of a Compositional Form.* Trans. Valentina Zavarin and Susan Wittig. Berkeley: University of California Press, 1973. Structuralist analysis of "point of view" on differing "planes" of an artistic work.

Wheelwright, Philip. *Metaphor and Reality.* Bloomington: Indiana University Press, 1962. "Diaphor" and "epiphor" in semantic tension.

IV. Hermeneutics as History of Biblical Interpretation

A. Primary Sources

Augustine (Aurelius). *On Christian Doctrine.* Trans. D. W. Robertson Jr. New York:

Liberal Arts, 1958. Theory of *signum* and *res*. Biblical interpretation influenced by the rules of Tyconius.

Ernesti, Johann August. *Elements of Interpretation*. Trans. Moses Stuart. New York: Dayton and Saxon, 1842. Another English translation: *Principles of Biblical Interpretation*. Trans. Charles H. Terrot. 2 vols. Edinburgh: T & T Clark, 1832-1833. "Grammatical" school of biblical interpretation. General hermeneutics is restricted to grammatical rather than historical approach; special hermeneutics is theological.

Gilby, Thomas, ed. *St. Thomas Aquinas: Theological Texts*. Durham, N.C.: Labyrinth, 1982. See especially pp. 15-21 for key texts relating to biblical interpretation.

Oesterle, Jean T., trans. *Aristotle: On Interpretation (Peri hermeneias). Commentary by St. Thomas and Cajetan*. Milwaukee, Wisc.: Marquette University Press, 1962. Thomas's commentary on Aristotle serves as a philosophical foundation for the biblical interpretation of Catholic scholasticism, as well as scholastic theology.

Origen. *Origen: On First Principles*. Trans. G. W. Butterworth. London: S.P.C.K., 1936. Threefold sense of Scripture. Origen was both the founder of textual criticism and the grand master of allegorical exegesis.

Spinoza, Benedict de. *A Theologico-Political Treatise*. Trans. R. H. M. Elwes. New York: Dover, 1951. Rationalist approach to biblical interpretation, advocating freedom of thought and speech and religious liberty.

Turretin, Francis. *The Doctrine of Scripture: Locus 2 of Institutio Theologiae Elencticae*. Ed. and trans. John W. Beardslee III. Grand Rapids, Mich.: Baker Book House, 1981. Classic Reformed source for Old Princeton School doctrine of plenary verbal inspiration of Scripture.

B. Secondary Sources

Aldridge, John W. *The Hermeneutic of Erasmus*. Richmond, Va.: John Knox, 1966. Erasmus deals with the sources through a "philological critical method, implemented by an historical critical approach."

Daniélou, Jean. *From Shadows to Reality: Studies in the Typology of the Fathers*. Trans. Dom Wulstand Hibberd. London: Burns and Oates, 1960. Broad notion of typology. Rehabilitation of Origen and advocacy of patristic interpretation.

_____. *Origen*. Trans. Walter Mitchell. New York: Sheed and Ward, 1955. Began revival of modern historical studies of Origen and the central role of his allegorical method in the history of biblical interpretation.

Ebeling, Gerhard. "The New Hermeneutics and the Early Luther." *Theology Today* 21 (1964-65): 34-46. Correlates Luther's hermeneutical shift with that of contemporary phenomenological hermeneutics.

_____. *The Word of God and Tradition: Historical Studies Interpreting the Divisions of Christianity*. Trans. S. H. Hooke. London: Collins, 1968. See especially the essay " 'Sola Scriptura' and Tradition" (pp. 102-47), which challenges the dichotomy between Protestant and Catholic views on the formation and authority of Scripture.

Farrar, Frederic W. *History of Interpretation*. 1886; reprint Grand Rapids, Mich.:

Baker Book House, 1961. Standard nineteenth-century summary; view of the relationship between theory of inspiration and method of interpretation is especially valuable.

Frei, Hans W. *The Eclipse of Biblical Narrative: A Study in Eighteenth and Nineteenth Century Hermeneutics.* New Haven, Conn.: Yale University Press, 1974. Traces the major shift in biblical interpretation from the precritical era through D. F. Strauss.

Grant, Robert M., with David Tracy. *A Short History of the Interpretation of the Bible.* Rev. ed. Philadelphia: Fortress, 1984. Grant's historical and Tracy's theological erudition in introductory and summary form.

Hanson, R. P. C. *Allegory and Event: A Study of the Sources and Significance of Origen's Interpretation of Scripture.* Richmond, Va.: John Knox, 1959. Argues for a narrower definition of typology and a broader definition of allegory than Daniélou's. Comprehensive study of Origen's exegesis.

Klassen, William. "Anabaptist Hermeneutics: The Letter and the Spirit." *Mennonite Quarterly Review* 40 (1966): 83-96. Anabaptist conflicts with Spiritualists and biblicistic Swiss Brethren; special attention to the Pilgrim Marpeck.

Longenecker, Richard N. *Biblical Exegesis in the Apostolic Period.* Grand Rapids, Mich.: Eerdmans, 1975. Particular focus on use of rabbinic methods of exegesis.

Patte, Daniel. *Early Jewish Hermeneutic in Palestine.* Missoula, Mont.: Scholars, 1975. Contrasts classical and sectarian Jewish hermeneutics, arguing that the Dead Sea Covenanters utilized "a radically different hermeneutical structure" from the classical *halakah-haggadah.*

Preus, James Samuel. *From Shadow to Promise: Old Testament Interpretation from Augustine to Young Luther.* Cambridge, Mass.: Harvard University Press, 1969. Using focal concept of "promise," argues for "hermeneutical divide" in Luther's *Dictata super Psalterium.* Note also extensive discussion of medieval hermeneutics.

Runia, Klaas. "The Hermeneutics of the Reformers." *Calvin Theological Journal* 19 (1984): 121-52. Defends hermeneutics of the Reformers as conforming to the Bible's understanding of itself.

Smalley, Beryl. *The Study of the Bible in the Middle Ages.* 2nd ed. Oxford: Blackwell, 1952. The classic historical introduction to medieval biblical interpretation.

Stein, Stephen J. "Quest for the Spiritual Sense: The Biblical Hermeneutics of Jonathan Edwards." *Harvard Theological Review* 70 (1977): 99-113. Analyzes continuities and discontinuities between Edwards's creative exegesis and the traditional Protestant biblical interpretation of his time.

Steinmetz, David C. "The Superiority of Pre-critical Exegesis." *Theology Today* 37 (1980): 27-38. Critique of historical-critical method. Argues for a renewed understanding of precritical exegesis as a valid approach to interpretation with its own controls.

Stines, James W. "Language Theory and Hermeneutics in the Thought of Horace Bushnell." *Perspectives in Religious Studies* 7 (1980): 134-50. Argues for centrality of Bushnell's theory of language in his theology and for continuities between

Bushnell, "the later Wittgenstein," and existential hermeneutics.

Terry, Milton Spenser. *Biblical Hermeneutics: A Treatise on the Interpretation of the Old and New Testaments.* New York: Phillips and Hunt, 1883. Standard text on Protestant biblical hermeneutics with extensive discussion of history of biblical interpretation.

V. Contemporary Biblical Hermeneutics

Alter, Robert. *The Art of Biblical Narrative.* New York: Basic Books, 1981. Formalistic literary approach to narrative in the Hebrew Bible. Special emphasis on "type-scenes."

_____. *The Art of Biblical Poetry.* New York: Basic Books, 1985. Formalistic approach to poetry of the Hebrew Bible emphasizing parallelism. "Hidden repetition" of parallelism points to "an increment of meaning."

Barr, James. *Old and New in Interpretation: A Study of the Two Testaments.* London: SCM Press, 1966. Critique of revelation-centered approaches to biblical theology.

Bartsch, Hans Werner, ed. *Kerygma and Myth: A Theological Debate.* Trans. Reginald H. Fuller. New York: Harper & Row, 1961. Bultmann's famous programmatic essay on demythologizing, with critical essays.

Berkouwer, G. C. *Holy Scripture.* Trans. Jack B. Rogers. Grand Rapids, Mich.: Eerdmans, 1975. Biblical interpretation and authority from perspective of conservative Reformed dogmatics.

Blackman, E. C. *Biblical Interpretation.* Philadelphia: Westminster Press, 1957. Moderate historical-critical approach, directed especially toward practical application.

Brown, Raymond E. *The Sensus Plenior of Sacred Scripture.* Baltimore: St. Mary's University, 1955. Exegetical background and hermeneutical defense of *sensus plenior* as "additional, deeper meaning intended by God but not clearly intended by the human author, which is seen to exist in the words of a biblical text . . . when they are studied in the light of further revelation or development in understanding of revelation" (p. 92).

_____. "What the Biblical Word Meant and What It Means." In *The Critical Meaning of the Bible.* New York: Paulist, 1981. Historical-critical method recovers literal sense of Scripture, which has priority over legitimate "derived senses."

Bultmann, Rudolf. *Essays Philosophical and Theological.* Trans. J. C. G. Grieg. New York: Macmillan, 1955. Translation of the second volume of the four-volume German edition of Bultmann's collected essays. Other selected essays in *Existence and Faith: Shorter Writings of Rudolf Bultmann.* Ed. and trans. Schubert M. Ogden. London: Hodder & Stoughton, 1961. See especially Bultmann's essay "The Problem of Hermeneutics," in *Essays Philosophical and Theological,* pp. 234-61. Biblical hermeneutics as textual exegesis according to the historical-critical method, which involves preunderstanding and necessitates demythologization.

_____. *History and Eschatology.* New York: Harper, 1957. 1955 Gifford Lectures. All historical interpretation involves "preunderstanding."

Carson, D. A., and John D. Woodbridge, eds. *Hermeneutics, Authority and Canon.*

Grand Rapids, Mich.: Zondervan, 1986. Scholarly essays from conservative evangelical and fundamentalist perspectives.

Cate, Robert. *How to Interpret the Bible.* Nashville: Broadman, 1983. Popular introduction to the critical study of the Bible from a Baptist theological perspective.

Childs, Brevard S. *Biblical Theology of the Old and New Testaments.* Minneapolis: Fortress, 1993. Comprehensive biblical theology from a canonical perspective.

_____. *Introduction to the Old Testament as Scripture.* Philadelphia: Fortress, 1979. Development of a "canonical approach" to Old Testament interpretation.

_____. *The New Testament as Canon: An Introduction.* Philadelphia: Fortress, 1985. Extension of canonical hermeneutics to New Testament interpretation.

_____. *Old Testament Theology in a Canonical Context.* Philadelphia: Fortress, 1986. Canonical approach provides "a new method of theological reflection" for Old Testament theology.

Croatto, J. Severino. *Biblical Hermeneutics: Toward a Theory of Reading as the Production of Meaning.* Trans. Robert R. Barr. Maryknoll, N.Y.: Orbis, 1987. Extension and application of Ricoeur's hermeneutics to liberation thelogy in South America.

Culpepper, R. Alan. *Anatomy of the Fourth Gospel: A Study in Literary Design.* Philadelphia: Fortress, 1983. Parade example of the application of modern narrative criticism to a New Testament text.

Dunn, James D. G. "Levels of Canonical Authority." *Horizons in Biblical Theology* 4 (1982): 13-60. Dunn's response to recent canonical hermeneutics.

_____. *Unity and Diversity in the New Testament.* London: SCM Press, 1977. Argues for differing levels of scriptural authority in response to diversity of New Testament doctrine.

Ellis, E. Earle. *The Old Testament in Early Christianity.* Tübingen, Germany: J. C. B. Mohr/Paul Siebeck, 1991. Criticizes traditional tripartite view of formation of Old Testament canon and emphasizes Jewish hermeneutical patterns in New Testament biblical interpretation.

_____. *Prophecy and Hermeneutic in Early Christianity.* Grand Rapids, Mich.: Eerdmans, 1978. Essays focusing on the office of early Christian prophets and their "pneumatical" exposition of Scripture.

Funk, Robert W. "Saying and Seeing: Phenomenology of Language and the New Testament." *The Journal of Bible and Religion* 24 (1966): 197-213. Applies phenomenology of language to the parables of Jesus and the Pauline letters.

Keegan, Terence J. *Interpreting the Bible: A Popular Introduction to Biblical Hermeneutics.* New York: Paulist, 1985. Introductory survey focusing on contemporary hermeneutical trends in biblical scholarship.

Kelber, Werner. *The Oral and Written Gospel.* Philadelphia: Fortress, 1983. "Parabolic hermeneutic" of Mark versus "oral hermeneutic" of Paul.

LaSor, William S. "Prophecy, Inspiration and *Sensus Plenior.*" *Tyndale Bulletin* 29 (1978): 49-60. Defense of *sensus plenior* from evangelical Protestant perspective.

McCown, Wayne, and James Earl Massey, eds. *Interpreting God's Word for Today:*

An Inquiry into Hermeneutics from a Biblical Theological Perspective. Anderson, Ind.: Warner, 1982. Essays on contemporary hermeneutics from a Wesleyan perspective.

McKim, Donald, ed. *A Guide to Contemporary Hermeneutics: Major Trends in Biblical Interpretation.* Grand Rapids, Mich.: Eerdmans, 1986. Diverse collection of articles with large representation of conservative evangelical Protestants.

McKnight, Edgar V. *Meaning in Texts: The Historical Shaping of a Narrative Hermeneutics.* Philadelphia: Fortress, 1978. Relates philosophical hermeneutics and structuralism to New Testament narrative.

Mickelsen, A. Berkeley. *Interpreting the Bible.* Grand Rapids, Mich.: Eerdmans, 1963. Strongly linguistic approach stressing grammar; conservative lexical theology.

Nida, Eugene A. *Toward a Science of Translating: With Special Reference to Principles and Procedures Involved in Bible Translating.* Leiden: E. J. Brill, 1964. Advocates dynamic equivalence approach. Also see discussion of "meaning," pp. 30-119.

Olthuis, James H., with Donald G. Bloesch, Clark H. Pinnock and Gerald T. Sheppard. *A Hermeneutics of Ultimacy: Peril or Promise?* Lanham, Md.: University Press of America, 1987. Statement and evaluation of Olthuis's proposal synthesizing some of the text-centered strands of philosophical hermeneutics, linguistic philosophy and a contemporary Reformed doctrine of Scripture.

Osborne, Grant R. *The Hermeneutical Spiral: A Comprehensive Introduction.* Downers Grove, Ill.: InterVarsity Press, 1991. Detailed survey of general hermeneutics and genre analysis from an evangelical perspective. Advocates ten-step model of biblical interpretation.

Packer, J. I. "Infallible Scripture and the Role of Hermeneutics." In *Scripture and Truth.* Ed. D. A. Carson and John D. Woodbridge. Grand Rapids, Mich.: Zondervan, 1983, pp. 325-56, 412-19. A rationalistic evangelical account of the hermeneutical process and critique of modern Protestant and Catholic alternatives.

Perrin, Norman. *Jesus and the Language of the Kingdom: Symbol and Metaphor in New Testament Interpretation.* Philadelphia: Fortress, 1976. Interpretation of kingdom of God and parables of Jesus in modern New Testament hermeneutics.

Pinnock, Clark H. *The Scripture Principle.* San Francisco: Harper & Row, 1984. Moves away from rigid fundamentalism to more canonical approach, though still retains inerrancy label. Antiliberal polemics.

Poland, Lynn M. *Literary Criticism and Biblical Hermeneutics.* Decatur, Ga.: Scholars, 1985. Analyzes new literary approach to biblical interpretation and proposes a "model of contextual inquiry."

Ramm, Bernard. *Protestant Biblical Interpretation: A Textbook of Hermeneutics for Conservative Protestants.* 3rd ed. Grand Rapids, Mich.: Baker Book House, 1970. Argues for the "literal-cultural-critical method" as "the historic Protestant" method.

Ricoeur, Paul. "Biblical Hermeneutics." *Semeia* 4 (1975): 29-148. Applies his theory of metaphor to biblical parables; religious language as "limit concepts" that qualify poetic redescription.

_____. *Essays on Biblical Interpretation.* Ed. Lewis S. Mudge. Philadelphia: Fortress, 1980. Selected essays demonstrating the implications of Ricoeur's hermeneutics for modern theology (especially Bultmann and Moltmann) and the understanding of religious language.

Russell, Letty M., ed. *Feminist Interpretation of the Bible.* Philadelphia: Westminster Press, 1985. Contemporary introduction to feminist issues in biblical interpretation.

Sanders, James A. "Hermeneutics." In *Interpreter's Dictionary of the Bible.* Supp. vol. Ed. Keith Crim. Nashville: Abingdon, 1976, pp. 402-7. Overview of hermeneutical discussion since Bultmann. Particular emphasis on Sanders's contextual version of "canonical hermeneutics."

_____. *Torah and Canon.* Philadelphia: Fortress, 1972. Argues for a "canonical criticism" based on historical, social and cultural identity.

Schökel, Luis Alonso. *The Inspired Word: Scripture in the Light of Language and Literature.* Trans. Francis Martin. New York: Herder and Herder, 1972. Approaches biblical hermeneutics through philosophy of language and literary analysis within a Catholic dogmatic framework. See especially pt. 4, "The Inspired Work," pp. 255-305.

Sheppard, Gerald T. "Biblical Hermeneutics: The Academic Language of Evangelical Identity." *Union Seminary Quarterly Review* 32 (1977): 81-94. Explores the function of biblical hermeneutics within evangelicalism in the United States.

_____. "Canon Criticism: The Proposal . . . and an Assessment for Evangelical Hermeneutics." *Studia Biblica et Theologica* 4 (1974): 3-17. An evaluation of Childs's early work by one of his students.

Smart, James D. *The Strange Silence of the Bible in the Church.* Philadelphia: Westminster Press, 1970. Describes the hermeneutical problem of the meaning of the Bible in relation to the separation between the church and critical scholarship.

Spencer, Richard A., ed. *Orientation by Disorientation: Studies in Literary Criticism and Biblical Literary Criticism Presented in Honor of William A. Beardslee.* Pittsburgh, Penn.: Pickwick, 1980.

Stuhlmacher, P. *Historical Criticism and Theological Interpretation of Scripture.* Trans. Roy A. Harrisville. Philadelphia: Fortress, 1977. Argues for a "hermeneutics of consent" to overcome weaknesses of historical-critical method.

Thiselton, Anthony C. *New Horizons in Hermeneutics.* Grand Rapids, Mich.: Zondervan, 1992. Advanced textbook surveying theories of interpretation and reading and discussing their implications for contemporary biblical hermeneutics.

_____. *The Two Horizons: New Testament Hermeneutics and Philosophical Description, with Special Reference to Heidegger, Bultmann, Gadamer and Wittgenstein.* Exeter, U.K.: Paternoster, 1980. Clarifies the implications of modern philosophical hermeneutics for Protestant New Testament interpretation. Argues for broader appropriation of philosophical hermeneutics than is found in Bultmann.

Virkler, Henry A. *Hermeneutics: Principles and Processes of Biblical Interpretation.*

Grand Rapids, Mich.: Baker Book House, 1981. Focuses on practical application from a psychologically informed, conservative evangelical perspective. Argues for "principlizing" the narratives and crossculturally translating the commands of Scripture.

Westermann, Claus, ed. *Essays on Old Testament Hermeneutics.* Trans. and ed. James Luther Mays. Richmond, Va.: John Knox, 1963. Collection of midcentury essays from major German historical-critical scholars (including von Rad, Bultmann, Noth, Zimmerli, Wolff, Eichrodt).

Index of Authors

Index of Subjects